Patience...
Miracle
in Progress

by Sue Winget

Randall House Publications
P.O Box 17306
Nashville, TN 37217

Acknowledgment

Although there are many to whom I owe a sense of gratitude, I am indebted to Professor E. Dean Beven at Baker University. His sensitivity and overwhelming dedication to this book are deeply appreciated. Without his help on the final drafts, along with the proof-reading of Carol Kirchmer and Sharon Germes, this book may never have become readable.

Patience...
Miracle
in Progress

© Copyright 1988
Randall House Publications
Nashville, TN 37217
ISBN 0-89265-132-6

Author's Preface

I have always felt this is the Lord's story and His book. I feel privileged that He has chosen me to live and tell it. May He alone be praised.

His Servant,

Sue Winget

Dedication

*To a faithful Lord without whom this
book would have never been.*

CHAPTER 1

The sun was making its morning debut as Gary, my husband, yelled out another wake-up call, hopeful he might get me to roll out of my all-too-comfortable bed. It was Father's Day, June 17th, 1983; a special day for the dad of our household. I was feeling very guilty for not prying myself and our children out of bed to greet him on his day with a Father's Day breakfast and, at the very least, with hugs and kisses before he rushed out the door to begin what usually was one of the busiest days in a pastor's family. Gary had been the pastor of the First Baptist Church of Dodge City for only the past three months. This particular Sunday morning, Gary, too, was having trouble dragging himself off to the church, so it was easier for him to be patient with my slow and lazy morning start. We had just gotten home from a long trip to Chicago.

Gary was working toward his Doctor of Ministry

degree through Northern Baptist Seminary. To continue working toward this goal, he had to attend a class offered in the middle of June. Gary had been reluctant to leave me at home with all the home pressures of just caring for our three children, because of the added strain I had been under from our recent move to Dodge City. I had been feeling dizzy and lightheaded, and I ached in my joints; I felt much like I was suffering from a case of the flu. This condition was not constant, but would come upon me several times a week. When I felt this way, I would just go to bed for the day, and the symptoms would disappear and I would again feel fine.

Gary was mostly concerned that I seemed so tired all the time, although I felt that this and the other problems were just the normal condition any red-blooded housewife suffers after dismantling one home, trying to organize another, and uprooting my children and myself from our eight-year stay in our old home in Wellsville, Kansas. However, after much debate, and an offer to house-sit in Chicago for the week, I found it hard to fight Gary's persistent argument that I should accompany him on his journey to the Windy City. It was hard to fight the people in the church who had joined in Gary's crusade to give me a brief and much-needed rest. With more than a dozen new friends' strong encouragement to go with Gary and get away for a few days, we finally decided to shuffle the children between grandparents and friends back in Wellsville, since the children were not too well-acquainted with Dodge City people yet.

A couple in our new Dodge City church, the Marshalls, had called their son and daughter-in-law, Tom and Judy Marshall, who lived in the Chicago area and with whom Gary and I had shared our college experience fifteen years earlier. Judy had made arrangements for us to stay at the home of her brother, Dan Ford, while his family was on vacation. Judy and Dan's sister, Carol Bingle, had been my close friend and college roommate. When we were to be in Chicago, Carol, Judy, and Dan's parents, the Jim Fords, were to house sit with us.

Our brief stay was heavenly, for me. Gary spent the week with his nose hidden in his books, and I spent mine with my nose hidden in the pillows, catching up on my much-needed rest.

Gary became alarmed that I was sleeping so much, especially when there was a shopping center and a K-Mart very close by in which I showed no interest. I tried to assure him I was just taking advantage of my days off with no offspring responsibilities.

Gary continued to be concerned as we left Chicago. An inner feeling kept telling him I was not all right. He quizzed me so much about how I was feeling that I became angry with all the questions. He was seeing something that even I couldn't see within myself.

We had arrived home Saturday night, and our brief retreat to Chicago was over. We had collected Shawn and Shannon from their grandparents on our way back to Dodge City. Though we had all had a good time, we were content to be back together and in our own separate bunks.

Sunday morning came too soon. We were running later than usual for Sunday School. The thought that the bus would be here soon to pick up the children was racing around in my head as I was struggling to clear my eyes from the night's sleep. Gary had already gone to the church.

As I continued to struggle to remove the cloudy film from my eyes, I soon found my attempts to do so were futile. The cloudy film covering my eyes wouldn't seem to budge as I sleepily tried to blink it away. I had the same feeling one has when walking in a dense fog on a rainy day. I kept blinking my eyes, even washing my face, trying to get rid of the fog.

This had happened to me twice before, and it only lasted half an hour or less, so I had no reason to believe it would be any different today. It was probably caused by the fatigue of traveling the long distance from Chicago

3

to Dodge City.

I tried to push the problem out of my mind by busying myself with getting ready for church. Just keeping the children working toward that goal kept my mind and hands busy. I kept telling myself I would have to wait until the inconvenience of my eye trouble passed.

The children soon were off to church on the church bus, but the fog in my eyes didn't seem to be passing as quickly as before. I had been sure it would be gone by the time they left. I knew it was unsafe for me to even attempt driving to church, but I was more concerned that Gary would hear of my problem before church was over.

I had learned in our fifteen years in the ministry to at least try to shield Gary from any unnecessary home problem before the church services if at all possible. This helped him concentrate more on his sermon and his other church responsibilities. I always had the opportunity to unload my gripes and problems at a time when he had fewer things crowding his mind. I knew I would be all right; in fact, I found the situation almost laughable. Though maybe it was not appropriate to make light of my present symptom, it was the only way I could cope with this condition at this time; however, I was concerned that Gary wouldn't be laughing once he found out.

My plan for secrecy didn't work. I had already called and asked my neighbor, Phyllis Stephenson, for a ride to church when Shannon, my ten-year-old daughter called. She needed a forgotten accompaniment tape from home immediately. Being a singer, I knew first-hand the frustration of having a missing tape just before a performance. Shannon and I had done a lot of singing together. As I talked to her on the phone about her problem, my mind drifted for a moment. I had a continuing desire to cut a record album within a year; maybe Shannon could do it with me. My mind was quickly snapped back to reality....

"Mom! I need my tape now," she pleaded. "I can't," the words slowly came out of my mouth. "Why?" Shannon queried.

4

I reluctantly and briefly explained to her why I couldn't bring the tape. Since she was calling from her dad's office, a very worried Gary came home to get the tape and check on me. I assured him that Shannon, needing her tape, was in far worse shape than I. I convinced him, as I had convinced myself, that I would be all right in a short time. It was just a passing eye problem and I would see him at the church shortly.

An unsure Phyllis picked me up on her way to church. When we arrived at church and entered the building, she questioned whether I would be all right on my own. My eyes seemed to be getting worse, but I had too much pride to admit to myself or to anyone else that I needed help. I laughed and assured her I was just fine. Phyllis and I parted company, and she ran up the stairs to her Sunday School classroom. I turned to walk down the long, twenty-five foot hallway which would lead me to another stairway going down into the basement, where Gary's office was located. As I turned and looked in the direction of the hall, I was suddenly aware I couldn't see to the end of the corridor. I couldn't even see what was four feet ahead of me. My world had suddenly been swallowed up in a foggy, hazy cloud. Alone, I began to shuffle down the hall. People passed me, speaking in friendly chatter. I couldn't tell who they were, not having been in the church long enough to distinguish the difference between people's voices. Why had I let Phyllis leave me! The people all looked so hazy and fuzzy. I couldn't make my eyes focus on them. Why couldn't I ask anyone for help? Was it because I didn't know these people?

The fog seemed to be getting thicker by the second. I reached my hand over and touched the wall. Some of the panic drained from my weak body, and I was able to move my feet one step at a time. My whole body trembled as I inched my way down what seemed to be a never-ending hall.

It seemed an endless walk down that corridor with the knowledge that I would soon be coming to the stairway. I couldn't see it, but I could picture it in my mind. Afraid to trust in myself, knowing each step was bringing me closer to the stairs, I froze. My legs would no longer move. My heart pounded within me. I was certain it was setting off an alarm that everyone in the church could hear. My eyesight seemed to have gotten progressively worse with the tension of every step I took down that dark hall. I wanted to cry out for help, but nothing came out of my mouth. For the first time in my life, I was completely immobilized with fear.

Only a few short seconds passed, but it seemed like much longer. I stood tightly gripping the banister to the stairs, not knowing what to do next. Suddenly I was aware there was someone or something at the bottom of the stairs. The blurred form began speaking to me. It was a warm, feminine voice extending me a friendly, "Hi."

I was still frozen like a cube of ice in my present pose, tightly gripping the top of the banister that led down the stairway. At the bottom of the stairs there was a hallway leading into the basement. I strained to see if the person standing there was perhaps speaking to me. It was only six short steps down into the basement where the unknown person was standing, but my eyes wouldn't focus on the blurred form. I could only see a hazy outline of an image. If the unknown stranger hadn't uttered an audible word, I wouldn't have even known this creature-like blur was alive. Slowly and hesitantly I returned the "Hi."

Finally, out of the silence, from the unknown blur, came, "Mom?"

"Shannon, is that you?" I asked with a sigh of relief.

Her response sounded like a question as she uttered a soft, almost inaudible, "Yes."

"Please take me to your dad's office," I begged. I was very certain then that she must have been sent by my extremely nervous guardian angel.

Shannon had known from our phone conversation

6

earlier in the morning that I hadn't been feeling quite right, but my present strange behavior really concerned and puzzled her. She had also been deeply hurt that her own mother didn't even recognize her. My extremely sensitive, ten-year-old Shannon took our brief encounter on the stairway as a personal rejection. At her young age she couldn't understand what was actually happening to me; at thirty-five I was puzzled, too. I was also unaware that she had taken our meeting on the stairs so personally. She had always acted so grown-up. This time the ten-year-old in her had hidden the piercing hurt deep within her tender heart.

All the tension was slowly draining out of me as I reached out my hand and tightly grabbed her extended, much-welcomed hand. It felt strange for her to be helping me; that had always been my job. She led me down the stairs and through the door into the large Fellowship Hall. I didn't know whether anyone was watching us as we crossed the room hand in hand. Shannon led me into her dad's office and quickly left for her Sunday School class.

The church office complex is a cluster of rooms located off one end of the basement. The secretary occupies the outer office; behind her desk are three other offices. The middle room is where the supplies and office equipment, complete with copy machine, are stored. This room is very much in demand on Sunday mornings. Shannon had deposited me in a chair off to the side of the main door, right inside the secretary's office.

Dozens of people were warmly greeting me as they quickly slipped through the outer office disappearing into the supply room. They were unaware I was having any physical problems. Not having known these people very long, I was unsure what their response to this situation might be.

Gary could see my tension increasing as people spoke to me. It is difficult to try to learn three hundred new names and connect them with faces; it's easy for the congregation to learn the name of one new pastor and his

7

wife. This Sunday I wasn't able to get in focus even the few I did know by name. It soon became plain to me that I didn't know their individual voices at all. I was beginning to feel trapped and isolated within my private fog, and I was becoming embarrassed, not knowing who anyone was. I was unsure what my response should be to each greeting. Gary finally grabbed my hand and led me back into his office and shut the door.

Gary was trying to keep control of his emotions, reasoning within his thoughts, "The trip to Chicago must have been too much for Sue. Surely her eyesight would soon snap back, as it had always done before."

Before he had a chance to continue, his thoughts were interrupted by a rap at the door. Someone was asking, "Sue, would you be available to teach a class for a few weeks?" I was listening intently to each word she was speaking, trying to piece together facts and accents that would tell me who the woman was. Though she was standing beside my chair, I couldn't see her.

Thinking she must be the Superintendent of the Sunday School, I responded, "Yes, I'd be glad to." That was all she needed to hear; she quickly turned and exited.

Gary said in a very concerned tone, "You couldn't see her, could you? I'm taking you home and we're calling the doctor."

He announced to those people still gathered in the office that I wasn't feeling well. He was going to take me home and he would be back soon.

I was relieved to be home. Gary insisted, "I'm calling the doctor before I go back to church." The doctor instructed me to go to bed to see if my vision was better by Monday, and to definitely call his office if it hadn't improved.

This seemed to ease Gary's mind. He was sure that with a day or two of rest I would be fine again, as always. I soon forgot the panic I had experienced earlier in the hallway. At this point, no one was too concerned about the trouble with my eyes, blaming my present condition on our long trip from Chicago to Dodge City. The rest of the day I spent lying on the couch in our living room trying to follow the doctor's instructions: just waiting; waiting for the fog to go away, so I could see clearly once again.

While waiting for my doctor's appointment, I decided to try one of my own home remedies, taking my daily walk. In the past, walking had been a necessary activity for me. It was my way of fighting back at the neck and back pain which I had suffered since having been involved in two car wrecks.

My first wreck had been over ten years earlier in Ohio, where Gary was pastoring his first church. A man in his early twenties had smashed his car into the rear of my stopped car, causing my head to snap forward quickly and hard.

I had been wearing a hairpiece that day. I was to attend an all-day meeting, and to ensure that my hair piece stayed exactly in place, I anchored it down with a dozen additional hair pins.

The car hit us from behind with such force that my head whipped forward, throwing my well-secured hairpiece to the floor. It landed on the foot of my startled passenger. I was sure the police officer who reported the accident added a brief note to his report: "Woman involved in accident was in shock. Her hair was standing straight up in the air from the experience."

The other accident had occurred only two years earlier. I had been driving our van on an interstate highway during the busy rush-hour traffic in Kansas City, Kansas. My three children and another woman were with me in the van. I was driving faster than the rain-covered slick roads would allow, though I was driving the speed limit.

As I came to the crest of a hill, I suddenly realized the three lanes of traffic had come to a complete stop because of a wreck a mile up the interstate. There was no time or space for me to stop the van, or even to pray. I have always been certain the Lord took over driving the van at this point. When I pumped the brakes, the van began to hydroplane. It glided across the rain-soaked pavement as though it were on ice. The van spun around and slammed into an unyielding lamp post. This sent the van into the ditch backwards, burying the wheels deep in the mud.

We weren't the only vehicle unable to stop. Two others collided — a small car and a truck pulling a long trailer full of cattle, knocking them both off the highway. How I avoided hitting either one of them I am unsure, but I know the Lord did some fancy driving that day!

As I left the van to be towed away, I realized the ditch we had slid into sloped twenty feet to the bottom of a hill. Had the wheels not dug into the mud, the van would probably have rolled down to the bottom of that hill.

No one in the other vehicles was injured, but the woman in the van with us had been thrown out of her seat onto the floor. She was taken by ambulance to a nearby hospital, and the children and I rode in the police car.

I had been so concerned for the other woman and so busy making sure the children were all right that I hadn't noticed my right arm was just hanging from my shoulder, and my arm and hand had turned blue from aggravation of my old neck injury. My woman passenger sustained a neck injury also.

We went home that night feeling lucky to be alive and extremely fortunate. The injuries that were suffered that day, although painful, could have been much worse.

Pain became my frequent companion after these wrecks. A day without it seemed strange. It came often in different forms; sometimes a sharp pain at the base of my skull, often traveling down my spine and up the side of my head to my temple, causing a stabbing, sharp pain in my head.

I was caught in a cycle caused by pain. My pain was causing tension and the tension was causing me more pain. The pain made my mind dull, often robbing me of control of my life. My relief came only from the bottles of medication. It was much too easy to pop a pill, and many times I was unsure when I had taken the last pill.

I was already taking up to twelve aspirins a day. I realized I could become addicted to all the other pain pills and muscle relaxers I was taking. I began walking for exercise, and quit taking medication. Walking became one "pill" I found that would help relieve my pain. I soon found that when my pain was at its worst, if I pushed past it and forced myself to walk, it at least helped relieve some tension, which in turn decreased the pain.

Not only had I gone through the ordeal with the car wrecks, but I had a lung problem. I had been to five different doctors and spent twenty days in the hospital just a year earlier. Thousands of dollars later, all that was discovered was that my lungs were not draining properly, something I was already aware of. One doctor believed I could possibly have Lupus erythematosus, a collagen disease which often affects connective tissue, leaving the body with no immunities. We were told it would take up to five years to confirm this diagnosis.

So it was natural for me, that Monday morning in Dodge City, to think of walking. I always felt better after a walk, and perhaps walking would relieve the eye problem I was having. Although my neck wasn't bothering me, I couldn't help wondering if there might be a connection. As Phyllis Stephenson and I had been walking together since our move to Dodge City, she consented to go walk with me Monday morning. She was hopeful, too, that our walk might relieve whatever was affecting my eyes. I thought my vision had improved a little from Sunday. The world around me didn't seem quite so dark.

We hadn't even walked a block when Phyllis found out rather quickly that I couldn't tell if a car was parked in my path or moving toward me. As our walk continued, she kept me from walking into over a dozen parked or moving cars. We both tried to hide our growing concern as we joked and laughed about my problem. Phyllis soon ended our walk with the statement, "You need the bed, not walking."

I was finding my eye problem very exhausting and stressful for my eyes as well as my head. Trying to focus on my fuzzy world was hard work. "I think you're right," I agreed without any protest.

Phyllis walked me home. She was anxious to make certain I arrived safely. There is only one house between the Stephenson's home and the church parsonage. Phyllis glanced back quickly to make sure I had made it up the driveway and into the house. She knew her morning would be a busy one — although she'd be doing something she always looked forward to—she was to watch her one-year-old, twin grandsons. Meanwhile, I had collapsed on our couch, drifting off to sleep.

CHAPTER 2

Summer was beginning to give off its heat, and it was good to rest under the coolness of the ceiling fan. Surely all I needed was just a restful sleep: Didn't that always solve everything?

I wasn't able to get an appointment with my doctor until three o'clock Monday afternoon, so I thought I would sleep my time away until I could see him. After two days of seeing my world as though I were looking through a thick cloud, I was beginning to feel a strain in both my eyes and my nerves. Seeing the world around me so blurred and foggy was causing my head to throb in response to the strain.

Two hours later I awoke to discover the right side of my body and face were numb and tingly. Gary had told me when he left the house in the morning that he was to have an important meeting Monday morning, and I was afraid my present condition didn't warrant interrupting it.

I was trying to keep the situation in perspective. I was keeping my emotions tightly controlled. My mind was dulled by the nagging ache in my head, and I wasn't thinking too clearly, so I phoned Phyllis, seeking her advice on the numbness. Even though my brain wasn't working quite up to par, Phyllis replied much as I had envisioned she might. "Hang up the phone and call the doctor, and see if you can't get an earlier appointment. I can't leave the twins or I'd take you. You better call Gary."

"I'll try to get an earlier appointment," I added, "but I won't call Gary. I don't think it's necessary to bother him, or that my present condition is anything that serious."

I hung up the phone and called the doctor's office. I was feeling a bit self-conscious; I couldn't help thinking Phyllis was over-reacting. I was only making the call because Phyllis was so concerned. While I was checking with the doctor's office, she was calling Gary's office, leaving an emergency message for him to call her back. Together, she and Gary's secretary, Earliene, had decided that Gary needed to be told of my new symptom.

Since I had decided not to be concerned about my condition, my call to the doctor's office sounded anything but urgent. I was finding it difficult to take this situation seriously. I wouldn't allow myself to believe anything life-threatening would happen to me. Still trying to be very much in control of my emotions, I reported my additional symptom to the doctor's nurse with all the enthusiasm of Howard Cosell.

Not detecting any sign of urgency in my voice, the secretary reported that the office would be extremely busy the entire day. The doctor wouldn't be able to see me any earlier than my scheduled appointment. I would have picked a day when all of Dodge City decided they needed to go to the doctor!

Being somewhat disgusted with doctors anyway, I decided to put everything on hold, when Gary came thundering through the door. He was breathless, his face visually disturbed, his blue eyes blood-shot and filled with anxiety. The lines in his forehead seemed deeper than usual. My attempt to make light of the situation did not erase the disturbed look in his eyes.

Something deep within me could feel his pained concern. In the past two years we had grown very close in our relationship. Realizing that all the pressures and strains of the church were pulling us apart, we had entered a critical phase in our ministry. We began pouring a lot of time and energy into "us." This was the reason Gary was not only worried about my condition; he was experiencing it, as if his own body were being affected. Over the last five years of our marriage he had seen me try to deal with much sickness and physical pain.

The frustration of just not knowing weighed heavily upon me. Though I had tried to hide these thoughts deep in my mind, they kept surfacing. I was angry with the Lord. Feeling He must somehow be enjoying my pain and suffering, I had silently slipped away from a close relationship with Him. I was putting the Lord on a shelf somewhere in the corner of my life, letting Him fit in whenever it was comfortable or convenient for me.

Though once my relationship to my Lord had been exciting and an adventure, I had lost contact with my first love, Jesus Christ. I had been much busier than He had ever intended me to be; too busy for a time of fellowship with Him. I had been off involving myself in church work, neglecting "Christ" work. I had become burned out, a common problem among those doing their "works" in order to achieve self-satisfaction and fulfillment, or to bring glory to their own particular church, rather than honoring the Lord through their church.

Though I was running away from the Lord because of my personal trials, Gary had been like a strong tree bending with the force of the gusty winds. Each stormy trial that came our way, he took seriously and with concern; but he never gave in to the pressures. I was perplexed, unable to find any answers, even through the doctors. I found it easier to deny having a health problem than to live with an unknown disease or condition. I wondered now what was in Gary's thoughts. As I looked at his face, I suddenly knew this was the expression Gary always had when he allowed his mind to dwell on what could possibly be wrong with me. I could sense his painful thoughts, though he tried to hide them. Something within me wanted to protect him, because I couldn't help feeling responsible for his anxiety.

It seemed forever as we waited for the hands of the clock to move slowly toward three. We sat silently, except for meaningless chatter. We both were trapped in our thoughts, questioning what was happening to me.

As we finally arrived at the doctor's office, I asked to wait out in the car until they called me into the office. I knew, especially because of all the patients he was to see that day, that my wait would be a long one.

It was a warm day in the mid-eighties. I was sure I would be more comfortable lying down in the seat of our car than sitting in the waiting room for an hour. Gary said, "I'll go sit in the office until they call your name; then I'll come and get you."

"That would be fine," I agreed.

My head was pounding harder with each beat of my heart. I guess my vision trouble, combined with the tension of seeing the doctor, was more stressful than I realized. I felt each beat of my heart echoing in my brain, like the bass drum beating in a band. I could count the beats as they grew louder and louder. "One, two, three, four. ONE, two, THREE, four. ONE, TWO, THREE, FOUR."

The afternoon was smoldering. Sitting in the car was becoming more unbearable by the moment. As the hot sun's rays beat down upon the car, the temperature inside kept rising.

Waves of nausea came over me with the intense pounding in my head. My strength was being drained, and I began to feel as though my whole body was weighted down. I grew limp, almost faint, as the pain and nausea took command of my body. Each time I moved I felt more nauseated. I lay as still as I possibly could. I felt powerless to get help; I prayed Gary would come quickly.

When Gary came to retrieve me from the car, he was alarmed and bewildered to find me in this weakened condition. He was unsure he could even get me into the office.

Dr. Trotter, a personal friend from our college days, took a quick look at me and suggested I belonged in the hospital where he could properly treat the increasing headache and nausea with injections. Gary was grateful for this news, as he had already been trying to decide how he would be able to care for me at home in this weakened condition.

At this point, the prospect of being hospitalized was very comforting, and the thought that relief was possible made the pain almost tolerable. I could hardly wait to get out of the doctor's office and make what I hoped would be a speedy trip to the hospital.

Gary, who was trying to organize his own thoughts, was a little rattled from the speed at which I was declining. He seemed momentarily unaware of the growing pain in my head and the intense feeling that I would lose last night's nachos from the nausea which I was fighting. Instead of the prompt trip to the hospital I envisioned, he drove home to keep the kids posted on events and to pack my suitcase for my hospital stay. I suppose at a time like this, his mind wasn't functioning correctly and the administrator in him took control of his actions.

Knowing he hadn't quite caught up with the fast-moving events that were taking place, and mostly because I was too sick to move, I remained yet again in the car, while he struggled with the packing.

Since we had only lived in the parsonage a short time, he didn't know where anything was stored. Those things that he was able to retrieve, with the help of

17

Shannon, were winter items, and generally undesirable for mid-June. Finally realizing the urgent need was not getting my things packed, but getting me to the hospital, Gary gave up looking for my clothes and took me to the hospital.

After consulting with our doctor, we were temporarily relieved to learn he felt my symptoms could possibly be caused by a severe migraine headache. Another doctor, Dr. Howell Johnson, was called in for consultation, and the men agreed that a CAT scan should be run that evening.

The injections the doctor prescribed earlier in the day didn't deaden the pain. The nausea was increasing with every move of my head. I was feeling more and more disoriented, which I attributed to the medication I was receiving. The slightest move caused me to vomit.

Knowing I was in competent hands, Gary hoped I would drift off into a much-needed sleep. He was sure this would provide relief. Thinking I would perhaps sleep more quickly if he left, he slipped out to check on things at home. Our youngest son, Jason, was expected back from Wellsville Monday evening.

After living in Dodge City three months, Jason still was having a great deal of difficulty adjusting to our move from the only home he had ever known, Wellsville. He was definitely suffering from a severe case of homesickness.

We knew it might have been unwise to let him stay there in Wellsville while Gary and I were in Chicago, but he was so content and excited about staying with Gary's former secretary, Vesta Burbank, on her farm, that we decided to let him do it.

Very different from his older brother Shawn, our Jason loved to put those slick, slimy, wiggly worms on the end of his fishing pole, sit on the bank of a slow-moving creek, and watch frogs plop from the banks, leaving their giant water rings slowly reaching toward the shore.

His clever wit and continuously questioning spirit

could not change this slow-moving, unrushed guy. If his unique response didn't quickly win any unsuspecting victim over, one would soon be trapped, sinking slowly into those big, dark, brown, cocker spaniel eyes. That seemed to get him whatever he wanted. A lover to all ages was our Jason, a kid to remember.

He was having so much fun at Vesta's. He had become an honorary Burbank, and it was difficult to end his short vacation on their farm. To make matters worse, Vesta, too, was unwilling to loosen her grip on "her Jason."

Knowing his love for Vesta and her farm, we had consented to a few more days of his fishing and frolicking on the "Burbank banks" after our Chicago journey.

Many times over the past years, we had questioned whether the Lord had put Jason in the wrong place at birth. Maybe he was supposed to be dropped off at a pond instead of a parsonage. Mistake or not, we felt blessed to have him as a member of our "Winget flock." Nevertheless, we knew he would have a difficult time coming back to Dodge City, where contrary to Jason's wishes, we didn't live on horseback.

Now we had an additional problem for Gary to cope with. Jason was coming home and Mom was in the hospital— a prospect he continually feared.

Jason was a person who locked his feelings tightly within himself. Although he was extremely sensitive to those around him, he carefully kept his thoughts hidden within himself, often spending time alone with himself. He had allowed himself to get close enough to me to share those childhood secrets and thoughts.

My month's hospital stay, with lung trouble over a year ago, had left a scar on Jason that was constantly irritated by my unstable health. To be greeted with the news that I had been hospitalized yet again would just confuse him and reinforce his negative feeling about returning to Dodge City. There seemed no way to lessen the sudden blow he would be greeted with upon his arrival home. He had already begun the long journey home,

19

unaware of what he was to discover.

Gary knew the information would best be received from him. Gary had left me at the hospital with the purpose in mind of meeting Jason when he got home .

Jason arrived home, anxious to share his many tales with us all. Envisioned in his mind were the regular hugs and kisses he believed all fishermen receive when returning home after a long fishing trip, especially when one is nine years old and a dreamer. Instead of being met the way he expected, he was greeted by an overzealous and hyper sister, Shannon, bearing the latest hospital report.

He responded with anger and disbelief, feeling she was just teasing him as she often did, being a normal big sister. Within minutes, Gary was there to confirm the news, increasing Jason's anxiety over the whole situation. His exhilaration and excitement about his trip had been traded for fear, anger, and uncertainty.

CHAPTER 3

Continuing to feel a need to get back with me but being pulled by the situation at home; sensing very deeply the hurt Jason was experiencing, Gary yielded to an inner urge to return to the hospital as soon as possible.

As he drove the short two miles back to the hospital, he continued his petition before the Lord—hoping to find me much improved, resting comfortably, and free from pain.

Starting a new pastorate required much of Gary's time as well as a great deal of energy. This can be a very stressful time even under the best of conditions, and to have me become ill now was only adding weight to his already heavily burdened shoulders. Trying to keep things running smoothly at home, the church, and the hospital was creating an inner conflict for him. It was creating a tenseness and tightness within him. Though it is his caring nature to try to be everywhere he is needed, he could not be, as hard as he tried.

Gary was back before they took me for the CAT

scan. By then I was too weak to sit up in the wheelchair, so I was moved onto a gurney and wheeled down to x-ray. As the aide moved me through the halls to the elevator, I kept my eyes closed. I was fighting nausea, as the gurney traveled swiftly through the halls.

The intense pain in my head was continous now; the medication didn't seem to bring relief, but it only seemed to be causing my mind to be more confused. It was as though I were experiencing a weird psychedelic dream. The x-ray room appeared to be whirling around, almost as if I were on a fast-moving merry-go-round.

I was having a great deal of trouble understanding exactly what the technician was saying to me. I couldn't make my mind understand the words as they came from his mouth. It seemed as if he were speaking a foreign language. I understood the words, but they weren't being processed in my head correctly.

The technician strapped my head into a harness, and he told me to let him know if I was going to become ill. As I lay there on that hard, cold table, I prayed that the jerking movement of the machine wouldn't make me sick. All I could think was how embarrassing and what a mess it would be to vomit in the CAT scan! This thought alone gave me all the inner strength that was needed to avoid such a predicament.

The technician viewed me through the window from the adjoining room. He was certain that he would find proof in the scan I had suffered a massive stroke, though he was hesitant to share his suspicion with Gary.

As Gary stood by, watching with the radiologist, he began to give in to his hidden fear that I might have a brain tumor. This fear was eased by the attending doctor, who could just assure him nothing of this nature had appeared in the scan.

That night, I kept having a strange sensation. I felt like there was a dizzy, floating sensation within my head. I fought for sleep, but the pounding in my skull won out. Although it was difficult to lie motionless, it was necessary. The surges of nausea had taken control of my body, limiting any movement. The night seemed long and lonely as I drifted in and out of sleep, waiting for the relief of morning.

The night's sleep might have been hampered by the knowledge that Gary was to take me out of the hospital the next morning for a few hours, since a special eye test was needed. The only place this test could be conducted in western Kansas was in a town near by, Garden City.

The next day Gary came prepared for our short trip. Since our van had a rear seat that makes into a bed, he was sure I would be able to survive the trip without any difficulty. He forgot the first problem would be hoisting me into the van. Just plopping me in the nearest seat was a major undertaking. My husband is five feet ten inches tall and weighs over two hundred pounds, but he found it difficult to lift my five-foot, seven-inch, one hundred twenty-five-pound body, due to my increased limpness and lack of balance.

The trip was more difficult for me than Gary had ever imagined. By the time we arrived, I wondered how I would even have the strength to hold my head up for the examination. First the doctor's assistant did a normal eye examination. I found it exhausting to follow the simple directions as I strained to identify the letters. He then ran a test to see if my peripheral vision was affected. I had to push a button every time I could see a light appear. Because my mind was so clouded, I was concerned that the results from the testing would not be accurate. While Gary stood silently watching, he realized I couldn't see the light until it was directly in front of my eyes.

Gary worried that I was finding even the simplest task difficult, often impossible, to perform. His hopes had been lifted so many times, only to be dampened by no apparent answer. Would this time be just another in a series of dozens of dead ends?

By the time the tests were completed, Gary had to pour me into the van. I just lay on the floor, content with the knowledge there was no place to fall any further. This way, I assured him, they could just roll me out when we finally arrived back at the hospital in Dodge City.

The ride back was much rougher on the floor of the van, as I experienced every bump in the road from Garden City, but I was very content to just lie where I couldn't see the countryside flying by. The movement was more than my stomach would tolerate. I kept my "barf tray" very handy, and we both breathed a huge sigh of relief when Gary saw the Dodge City Co-op grain elevator off in the distance, with its large ear of corn painted on the side.

The trip to Garden City revealed somewhat frightening news. It indicated there were multiple lesions on both sides of the optic nerve. The doctor explained that this could be causing some pressure on the brain. We were told to start preparing for my transfer to Wesley Hospital, in Wichita. At the present time, the Dodge City doctors were unsure if I needed to be seen by a neurosurgeon or a neurologist.

Both Gary and I tried to belittle the situation in an attempt to hide our own individual alarm. I jokingly said, "I've got a bunch of holes in my head." I couldn't reveal my true fears, founded on an event that had happpened over fifteen years ago. I knew it was deeply etched within my early childhood memories.

My father had an older sister, Verna, whom I had been told many times I looked very much like. Being her "little likeness," she favored me over her more than twelve nieces and nephews. Since she was not married until she was forty, my position in her life was an important one. She was an extremely special lady to me; I revered and loved her greatly. Two years after her marriage, she died after an operation for a brain tumor, but her memory continued to live on in me. In my grandparents' eyes and hearts, I took the place of "their Verna."

Through my teen years I had not yet developed any lifetime goals of my own, so I envisioned myself living within hers. Like my aunt, I too would become a nurse. As

24

the years passed, I realized that although we looked much alike, we definitely had been created from different molds.

During my junior year in high school, I started having headaches. Because of my Aunt Verna's history of a brain tumor, tests had been run to check me for the same condition. My parents relived the horror of her death once more through the tests. We were all relieved when the tests came back negative.

Now as I lay in the Dodge City hospital room, the memory of Aunt Verna's death was once again filling my thoughts. Was I to have brain surgery too? A terror inside that was over fifteen years old kept echoing a threat: "You will never live through brain surgery." Was it fate that I had always been my aunt's "little likeness"? All these thoughts were racing through my mind, but I couldn't share them with Gary, at least not now.

My condition by evening had deteriorated. Gary was becoming increasingly perplexed: Each time he came to visit me, my condition had changed. Dr. Trotter and Dr. Johnson did a neurological check on me the following day and discovered my whole body was numb. My legs felt heavy and I could walk only with assistance. I had no sense of balance and I was having difficulty hearing. The decision was made. I definitely should go to Wichita. Dr. Barnett, a neurologist, would be contacted. The doctors assured Gary it was not yet an emergency that I get to Wichita, so I didn't need to fly in the air ambulance, unless I felt it necessary. I could also be taken in an ambulance. "Could we use our van?" Gary questioned. "It would be as comfortable as an ambulance." Since there was no emergency, the arrangement for getting me to Wichita would be left up to Gary.

To add to his already frustrated mind, there had been a death within our church family and the funeral was to be held on Wednesday, the day they wanted me to be in Wichita. I felt I was such an unnecessary added burden to Gary. I could sense his increasing frustration, although he was trying to hide it from me.

He was really undecided about how to transport me to Wichita, since there were three services and a family luncheon relating to the death. This would involve him until late in the afternoon. Wednesday morning before he began his busy schedule, Gary rushed into the hospital to let the doctors know he wouldn't be able to take me until late in the afternoon. He arrived while the doctor was in the room. Through the night my condition had continued to decline. My speech was slurred and I was having difficulty speaking. Dr. Johnson was now visibly concerned, and suggested Gary get me to Wichita as soon as possible.

This made Gary's decision about how to get me to Wichita more difficult. A funeral can't just be called off! When he got back to the church he made arrangements for Agnes Harris, a friend from church, to drive me to Wichita. She didn't want to drive our van, but she would pick me up at noon in her own car. Gary came quickly back to the hospital to share his plan with me.

I was unsure how I could tolerate riding in the back seat of a car: however, I didn't tell anyone. I was causing Gary so much concern and frustration already, and he was doing the best he could for me. I could also envision dollar signs in my mind when I thought about flying or taking an ambulance for the three-hour trip.

Part of a pastor's wife's concern is protecting her husband, if possible, from the many situations that come flying at him. It was hard to turn this role off as long as my mind was functioning at all; it just came as second nature to me.

Gary was trying to keep my parents, who live in Topeka, Kansas, posted on my changing physical condition. He was finding it increasingly more difficult even to keep those right there in Dodge City informed. He did arrange to have my mother and a sister meet me when I got to Wichita, knowing they would make sure I received the proper care until he arrived after the funeral.

Over the last two days I had begun to experience

increasing noise in my head and ears.

After Gary left for the day and Wednesday morning progressed, I was becoming more isolated in my own silent, lonely, shrinking world. I hated it there; there seemed to be no one but me.

The new world I was experiencing made me feel so lonely, so isolated from the world I was familiar with. As a rule, even before this experience I didn't like to be alone with myself. I guess it was because I didn't enjoy my own company. To avoid this unpleasant situation I usually found some busy work to do. This time I was forced to be alone with myself. I couldn't run, even from me.

I felt as though I were drifting, or falling down a long hall. I could see no ending to this seemingly eternal hallway. How I longed and prayed the Lord would send someone, anyone who could hold me, comfort me. It seemed I was drifting somewhere between those I knew and loved in life, and those gone before me in death.

I felt as if I were closer to those already gone before me, although I couldn't remember any of their names. The only one I could think of was Bob Stephenson, Phyllis' husband, but I had never met the man when he was living. I wondered if he would know me in death. Somehow I felt a bond with him, almost as if I were drifting to meet him.

Then my thoughts floated to my family. Could Gary live with my death? What about my children? Would they blame God? Would they ever see this was really a blessing from Him not to leave me this way? If only I could talk to them. I sobbed within myself....

I was beginning to lose the control of my arms and legs. They were moving as though they were free of the control of my mind. I was unable to talk. The words were stuck somewhere within my head. Meaningless disconnected words and sounds were all that would come out.

Gary had asked Phyllis if she would come to see me before I left. She had promised to come during the funeral and stay with me. Agnes and her friend, Margaret Marshall, another church member, were to take me to Wichita immediately following the service.

The graveside service was forty miles from Dodge City following the funeral, making Gary unsure just when he would get to Wichita. His mind was filled with all the necessary details, and his concern about me was almost too much for him to carry as he reluctantly pulled himself away to go to the funeral.

When Phyllis arrived at the hospital, she was dressed all in white. As she entered the room, I had no idea who she was. All I could see was the fuzzy outline of someone in white—possibly a nurse, but because of all the bizarre things I was experiencing I questioned for a brief second whether my visitor might be an angel. As I questioned, the silence was broken by the familiar sound of Phyllis' voice.

The account as viewed by Phyllis:

"Just entering the hospital caused a rush of emotions that brought back unpleasant thoughts and memories of Bob's death; I knew it was a place I couldn't avoid. It also brought uncertainty as to what I might find when I saw Sue. I was afraid. As I entered her hospital room I wasn't prepared for what I saw!

"I was surprised! Sue didn't recognize me as I entered the room: I didn't think she was that bad. She couldn't get out of bed—that scared me! I didn't want her to see my fear, because I didn't know how frightened she was. It was difficult to know just how she felt, because our communication was so limited. I wasn't sure Sue was functioning well enough to even be afraid. If she was, she might sense my fear, so I tried to hide my disbelief.

"Sue was having trouble hearing me, and couldn't understand what I was trying to say to her. She couldn't let me know what she understood.

"*I just wasn't prepared.* It was such a drastic change. Things usually change in a gradual, slow way. Yes, it was gradual, but I would have liked the process to be slower. It was gradual, but little things were happening within a two or three hour span of time. It wasn't gradual like a day here or there.

"I felt sure Sue was in the process of becoming a wheelchair victim. It didn't cross my mind at the time that she might die, but I was sure she would be severely physically handicapped.

"Not only couldn't she get out of bed without assistance, she couldn't see who I was; her speech was distorted and it didn't make any sense. She couldn't answer any of my questions.

"I asked, 'Are you frustrated?' I could see her frustration as she swung her arm, hitting the railing of the bed trying to communicate. I didn't ask her any more questions.

"I began to cry. Tears not for myself, but for my friend. I felt a combination of shock and concern. Shock over the situation I was facing. Concern for my friend. I felt such a helpless feeling."

She was the first of many people who would be totally unprepared for what they were to find. She walked over to my bed and gently took my hand. Fear swept through her whole body, as she tried desperately not to let me see the shock and dismay she was feeling inside. It was hard for her to believe it was me. She had just seen me a day and a half earlier, and the change was drastic; it happened too fast to even have time to question. As the tears began to stream down her cheeks, I lay there silently, unable to wrap my arms around her to comfort her. Too weak to share her tears, I could feel her intense pain. I wanted desperately to comfort her, but I was locked as a prisoner within my body. All I could do was pray for her.

I prayed, "Lord, you can't allow her to be hurt again." I questioned, "Was it really fair for me to have gotten so close to her? Could she cope with yet another illness after Bob's death?" These thoughts, however, didn't enter her mind. Her thoughts were filled with concern for me and anger with the Lord for what was happening. It seemed so unfair to her, so wrong.

She was still crying when she had to leave for her home. Her face was filled with helplessness and despair.

Phyllis left the room. My mind wandered back to the first day I met her. When we arrived at Dodge City, the people encouraged me to befriend Phyllis. Her husband, Bob, had died at the age of forty-four, just six short months before our arrival.

Bob had fought a one-year battle with stomach cancer. He was still an active deacon and adult Sunday School teacher when he died. The people in the church were still grieving his death when we arrived in Dodge City.

Phyllis only lived two houses from the parsonage, but she had been in Denver for spring break, missing our first Sunday as the new parsonage family. My first opportunity to meet her was a week later.

She was presiding over a women's group. As I looked about the room, the women were almost all seventy or eighty, with the exception of one woman who appeared to be in her early forties. She had short, blond, curly hair. I guessed her to be my height, five-seven or five-eight. I asked the church secretary, "Who is that woman, and why isn't she involved in a circle of younger women?"

"That's your neighbor, Phyllis Stephenson." Earliene explained further, "She likes to help with the older women's circle. She feels it's a ministry, and these women need her."

I went over to Phyllis' home later that day for a brief visit. We quickly found out, as Shannon so often says, "We shared the same weird sense of humor."

I am sure the Lord was keenly aware of my need for friendship in this new situation. Phyllis, too, was in need of a friend—someone who was not afraid of her grief, and who would allow her to share it openly. I too was grieving, but over something quite different. I was grieving over the death of our ministry in Wellsville.

30

I am not sure how we managed to overcome the barrier of my being her minister's wife; possibly because we were at very vulnerable phases in our individual lives. Our talks over the coffee cups soon took on a new dimension. I expressed my desire to find someone to walk with me, since I had left my walking partner back in Wellsville. Knowing she needed the exercise, she agreed to accompany me.

Phyllis was, and remained, very private in her grieving. I respected and kept those feelings confidential. On those rare moments when she did share, I tried to carefully and gently pull the hidden pain out of her, a little at a time. She was a woman strong in spirit and will. She soon discovered that I was, too. This German lady was not too strong for my spunky Irish spirit. I was not afraid of her grief, and I encouraged her to share it—at least with me.

I stayed her close companion as she relived the horror of Bob's illness and death through Jan her sister-in-law's battle with cancer. We felt a family bond as we stood by watching Jan, who was also Gary's cousin, lose her brave fight.

My concern was that Phyllis had been hurt so much over the last few years. I questioned, "What if I become ill again? Is it fair to her to be subjected to any more pain? Will she allow herself to begin a relationship with me, or is it fair for me to let her get close to me?" I couldn't help being afraid for her. She had lived through so much sickness and death already.

Was she able to deal with my illness if it recurred, especially when I was unsure of what it was? I often asked her this question, but she laughed it off, feeling it an unnecessary request. Neither of us was aware of how our new friendship would be tested.

CHAPTER 4

Following the funeral Gary conducted in Dodge City, he thought it necessary to gather all three of our children in his office to inform them what was taking place. He wanted to be honest, letting them know the seriousness of my condition, yet not frightening them. They needed to know that their mother could possibly have M.S. or something else very serious.

As Gary began to share the gravity of the situation it became too much for even him. As his grief poured out, the tears flowed. The children too began to share in his tears, uncertain of the future, and afraid of what it might bring.

Shannon and Jason were to go with Gary's parents, but Shawn insisted on going with Gary to Wichita. Being the oldest child, he not only was feeling a sense of responsibility toward me, but also wanted to be a support to his dad.

Trying to prepare them to see me before I left, he

tried to explain that I looked like a severe stroke victim. This didn't even begin to prepare them for the shock they were to feel.

After the funeral, Carol Kirchmer volunteered to stay with me in my hospital room the rest of the morning, until I was to be transported to Wichita. This is her account of the day:

"It was a Wednesday morning. I had to play for a funeral. It's a wonder I even played anything worthwhile. My friend was sick and in the hospital. I needed to see her, but I couldn't go to her. Neither could her husband. He was the officiating minister at the funeral and had to go to the burial service at a cemetery out of town. How frustrating!

"Sue and I became acquainted quite a few years ago and kept our friendship over the years. Then miraculously she moved to Dodge City as my pastor's wife in March. How wonderful!

"Now Sue was going to be close and I could talk to her whenever I wanted to or needed to. She understood me and what was happening in my life. On this day in June, 1984, it wasn't my life that I was concerned about. Sue had become extremely ill, and she was the one who needed someone to turn to. As soon as I finished playing, I rushed to find Gary and get firsthand information about how Sue was doing. As soon as he could get free, we went into his office.

"I was amazed at his strength and attitude that morning. I wanted to comfort him and say the right things to him, but instead, he comforted me. Gary told me Sue's condition and that she was to be taken to Wichita that afternoon. I asked him if anyone was with Sue right then, and he said there wasn't. I then asked him if it would be all right if I would go see her. He said that would be great.

"Tearfully, I hugged that big, dear man whose whole life was falling apart around him, but whose courage and faith were still strong. I stumbled to the car, and made the fastest trip to Humana Hospital that was possible without a siren and police escort. My thoughts were all jumbled as I cried out to God and prayed for Sue and Gary all the way to the hospital.

"I don't especially like hospitals, and this day I cringed as I entered the building, wondering what I would find when I finally got to Sue's room. It was a long walk from the elevator to the end of the hall and room #212. I prayed that God would prepare me for whatever I found.

"Evidently I hadn't given God enough time to prepare me, for I was totally amazed as I saw Sue the minute I walked into her room. 'Shocked' might be a more accurate word to describe my reaction. I was not expecting Sue to be in such a weakened condition.

"I called out to Sue to let her know I was entering the room as I approached her bedside hesitantly. My heart was in my throat, and I could hardly speak as I leaned over to give her a hug and kiss. Her face was distorted, and she struggled to get any words out of her mouth. One side of her face showed signs of paralysis.

"What should I do next? On the table next to Sue's bed was her lunch tray. Why wasn't Sue eating? Why wasn't the table over her bed so she could reach it? What was going on here? Anger started surfacing as questions that bewildered me came to my mind. I didn't understand what was happening.

"Finally, I asked Sue if she was hungry and wanted to eat. I nervously jabbered about the food items on the tray just to make small talk. Sue then told me she couldn't feed herself, and at that point I realized what shape she was in. This dear friend had no control over her hands, arms, or mouth. She had no eye-hand coordination to be able to make her hand pick up a fork and get a bite of food to her mouth, and she couldn't see well enough to know what to pick up if she had wanted to.

"I was beginning to get hold of myself enough to think clearly. I began feeding Sue her lunch, one slow bite after another. She hardly had control of her tongue and mouth, but somehow she managed to chew the food enough to swallow without choking. It was a tiring, frustrating, and slow process, but finally Sue felt she'd had enough.

"Now what? I again tried talking—mostly babbling, I'm sure—and then realized Sue was having trouble understanding my rapid speech as well as hearing me. Her eyes were closed most of the time—if open, nonfocusing, non-seeing, just randomly moving in no certain pattern.

"I tried to make Sue comfortable. I tried to reassure her and give her peace of mind about what was happening to her body. Finally, I told Sue I wanted to pray with her. I held her hands tightly and prayed earnestly for God to heal Sue.

"As we waited for the time for her to leave, we made idle and insignificant conversation. It was difficult for Sue to make her brain and mouth work together. What she wanted to say didn't always come out right.

"About 1:00 or so , Agnes and Margaret arrived to take Sue to Wichita. I was so relieved to see them, because I felt that maybe now we could get the process started of finding out what was wrong with Sue.

"Up to this point, I had only seen her physical limitations while she was lying in bed. Now it was time for her to get up, go to the bathroom, and get in a wheelchair to go downstairs to Margaret's car. Another surprise for me! Sue couldn't walk by herself, either, and had no sense of balance.

"A nurse came to help get her out of bed and into the bathroom. It took the strength of us both to hold Sue up and get her into the bathroom. None of us were expecting what we found. We couldn't believe how one person could be so well a few days before and now be so utterly helpless.

"We got her into a wheelchair and took her down to the emergency exit where Margaret's car was waiting. We were just getting Sue settled and into place when Gary and the kids arrived. Sue was hurting and wanted to get on with the trip, so we said our good-byes and the car left.

"Gary expressed his thanks to me for being with Sue and helping. I had nothing to say except I was glad I'd been there. Tears flooded my eyes as we hugged and he went on to finish his pastoral obligations. I again prayed that God would be with these dear people and that the doctors would find what was wrong with my friend Sue."

Two willing but uncertain ladies had accompanied me as I was wheeled out to their waiting car. Unsure of what they had gotten themselves into, they stood there with chalk-white faces. The task they had volunteered for seemed such a simple thing to do, but seeing me in this unexpected condition made them feel incapable of tackling this three-hour journey.

Carol was helping them get me into the back seat of the car, a difficult chore, when Gary and the children arrived, hopeful they would catch us before we left.

It was a painful experience for my children to see me in this condition. As they looked down on me lying in the back seat, unable to even acknowledge them, it made their fears more real and intense. There was so much I wanted to tell them, but I couldn't move. My arms and legs seemed to be weighted down by some unknown force. I tried so hard to talk to them, but nothing would come out. My mind was functioning at least part of the time, and I wished they could read my thoughts at that moment.

I couldn't help wondering if this would be the last time I would see any of these beloved people, and I couldn't even say good-bye to them. I wanted to tell them how much I loved them, and what special people they were. I needed to tell them not to be angry and blame the Lord. He wouldn't let this happen to them to ruin their lives. He'd make them stronger people because of this, if they'd let Him.

I wanted to hold them and let them know it was going to be all right. I had felt it always was a mother's job to kiss the little hurts that come along in life and make them go away. This seemed to be one time that I couldn't do it. I didn't like them seeing me in this condition.

They each tenderly kissed me on the forehead. The two youngest ones were filled with thoughts of how they personally might somehow be responsible for my illness. They thought perhaps if only they had been more obedient or helpful, or if we still lived in Wellsville, this would never have happened. Shawn aged several years as he stood there, feeling very responsible to be supportive and helpful in our first big family crisis.

The thoughts of our nine-year old, Jason, as he watched the car drive away were: "I had thought Shannon was lying when she told me Mom was in the hospital. I didn't believe her. I felt sort of scared when I saw Mom. I didn't know what to think. I thought people were blaming Shannon and me that Mom was sick. That made me mad at 'em."

I could feel the hurt from my family. I could almost envision them standing there watching the car slowly move from their sight. I felt so alone. Not only had I left my family, but I left the new friends I had in Dodge City.

Since I couldn't hear the conversation in the front seat, I continued to be confined to my own often confused thoughts.

CHAPTER 5

My thoughts drifted back to our ministry in Wellsville. I missed and needed those people so much right now. I felt so secure there after our eight-year ministry. Our children had just been babies when we first arrived. Shawn was five-years old. He had gone to kindergarten there. Shannon was three-years old and Jason was just a year old. The only life the two youngest children had ever known was in Wellsville.

I thought of our friends within the church family. I needed their prayers now! They had gone through so much with the Wingets. Our children had bladder and kidney birth defects. This had required nine minor surgeries in a year's time. Gary and Shawn each had emergency appendectomies. Shannon and Jason had their tonsils removed and I had a hysterectomy.

Our always-active children had managed to add eleven broken or fractured bones to our list. Shawn broke his foot four times and his collarbone once. He received two injuries while he was playing neighborhood football. He kept trying, though his attempts were unsuccessful, to convince me the sport wasn't dangerous. Shannon, our awkward one, followed her brother's example. She broke her foot two different times when she tripped. She also dislocated and broke her right thumb three times. Jason's bones must have been stronger, because he only had a broken arm when he fell from the top of the swing set.

I laughed within myself as I thought how it seemed that one of the Wingets was always on the list of those needing prayer. My mind stopped suddenly. I was reminded of my present situation when Agnes laid her hand on my arm. I struggled to hear what she was saying. Her mouth was moving, but I couldn't hear any sounds. Her face showed her concern; I strained unsuccessfully to give her a reassuring smile. She returned to her conversation with Margaret.

I continued to be trapped in my thoughts of Wellsville. My daily walks had been very important to me when we lived there. I had been the first person to achieve the goal of walking five hundred miles around the new Wellsville track. I walked one hundred and twenty-five times around the quarter-mile track. I trudged through rain, snow, and ice to achieve my goal. Many times icicles would form on my ski mask from my breath.

I made good friends with Anita McDanials, a woman from our church, who ventured into the cold with me. Gary, too, joined us on many days. Winter had never been a favorite time of year for me, but I learned to enjoy those brisk walks.

My singing was also a large part of my life in Wellsville. The people in the church had encouraged me to do concerts. Singing had been important in my life since my junior high years. I started taking voice lessons when I was in the seventh grade and continued through my college years. In the last few years, I began to think of my singing as a career, instead of a hobby. I was singing with accompaniment tapes, and I spent at least an hour a day working with my PA system getting the songs ready for my concerts. I wrote in a brochure advertising my concerts: "Through the years Jesus Christ has become the most important and vital person in my life. He has stood by me through physical pain and suffering; lifted me when I felt despair; taught me to laugh and cry with Him.

"In our world we are surrounded by broken hearts and pain. Life seems to pass by so quickly we often scarcely even notice the dull ache too often hidden deeply within our own hearts and in others.

"Christ has given me a passion to give His love and hope through song and sharing his messages taught to me through my life and family. One of my greatest joys in my life has been to be used by Him in this way...."

Before moving from Wellsville, I had been attending Baker University in Baldwin, Kansas. Though I was a graduate of Sterling College, also a Kansas school, I had been working on a Master's Degree in Liberal Arts from BU. I wondered as I lay in the back seat of the car if I would ever achieve my goal of graduating.

My body ached as I struggled to find a comfortable position. "I must lie still," I thought, "I'm only upsetting Agnes and Margaret." Agnes reached over the seat each time I attempted to move.

Somehow, because of all my squirming, Agnes realized that I was hot. She removed the blanket that had been put on me before we left Dodge City, untied my heavy robe, and then I was able to rest more comfortably.

My mouth felt dry, and I tried to run my tongue over my teeth and lips. My tongue felt thick and numb, as though I had just received a shot of Novocaine from the dentist.

I felt the metal wires on my teeth. "My braces," I thought. "Women my age shouldn't have braces." I began to recall why I had to have them...

My dentist found that my jaws were dislocated. This had been caused, perhaps, just by the way my bite was constructed, although my teeth were straight. My jaws had been clicking and popping when I would open my mouth. He was relatively sure my headaches and neck pain were caused from my jaws. He had called the condition T. M. J.

After my second car accident, I began having more difficulty with my face, as well as my neck and back. My jaws were becoming stiffer, and some days it was difficult for me to move my mouth. The dentist and orthodontist feared I might do permanent nerve damage, possibly perforating a ligament.

They suggested that I might be a candidate for a new surgical procedure, followed by wearing braces two and a half years.

The operation involved breaking the bone in the roof of my mouth. An incision would be made between the roots of my teeth and upper lip. The incision would continue over the palate on the roof of my mouth. The palate would be cut in two down the center.

A heavy-duty extension bar was to be attached to my back teeth. A tiny screw was in the center of the bar. While I was still in surgery, the bar was to be screwed apart, leaving a gap between my two front teeth. This hole would be closed later with the braces.

Once my jaws had been set correctly, the surgeon and orthodontist told me the only problem would be with my lower jaw. It would be protruding further from my face than my nose, which would make my face considerably out of balance. To correct this problem, they suggested that the lower jaw needed to have some of the chin bone shaved off.

The doctors said it would change my appearance somewhat. Gary did not want me to have the surgery and go through the pain. He was also concerned about my possible change in appearance. He wanted the same "model of wife" he had chosen at the beginning of our relationship.

I was not certain how I would look after the surgery: I was already experiencing pain in my neck and face. The possibility that it might be eliminated or lessened brought me new hope.

Though he still wasn't convinced, Gary allowed the surgery. He knew my strong desire to have the surgery, but he continued to have doubts.

I was scheduled as on outpatient. After re-evaluating my records, the surgeon called the night before the surgery. He felt it best to change the procedure on my chin. Another incision would be made at the bottom of my teeth. The lower part of my chin would be cut off about one inch. Three-eighths to half an inch would be removed from this section. The remaining piece of bone would be wired on to my chin.

The entire surgery took three and a half hours. There were ten anxious members of our church waiting with Gary and my mother. When I came out of surgery, my face was the size of a basketball. My mother didn't recognize me as they wheeled me from surgery to a room.

For a month, my food had to be ground up before I could eat. Because of Gary's negative feeling toward the surgery, I tried to bear my pain in silence.

After six months, I began to feel a difference. The pain from the surgery was slowly decreasing; so was the neck, back, and face pain. The surgery had been a success....

Suddenly the car pulled over to the side of the road and stopped. Agnes quickly ran around the car to relieve Margaret as the driver. As we drove off once again, suddenly I was aware that it was raining. Surprised that I could see anything so small, I lay and watched the drops softly land one by one on the window as if they were my own tears.

I found myself questioning whether the Lord was aware of what was happening to me, or if He even cared. Where was He all this time? I had never needed Him so much in my life and yet He seemed so distant. Wasn't my life about to end? At least He could let me feel His presence now.

I was reminded of a song written by Joyce Landorf. She had sung it at the end of her tape "Balcony People":

Hold me up–I cannot stand.
Wrap your love around my soul.
Well, I've no faith–so loan me yours.
I think I've lost my hope.
And if I'm to see anything of God's mercy and his
   grace,
Let me see it, oh child of God, on your dear face.

Well, joy and hope have ebbed away.
I cannot see tomorrow, much less today.
So hug me with your words.
Put your arms under mine.
Hold me up until I'm fine.
For if I'm to see anything of God's mercy or his
   grace,
Let me see it, oh child of God, on your dear face.

So gather roun–hold us up.
Alone we cannot drink this bitter cup.
We're sinking in such deep despair.
Come quickly now–life is more than we can bear.
Oh, if I'm to see anything of God's mercy and his
   grace,
Let me see it, oh child of God, in your dear face.

My attention was drawn back to the slowly falling rain. Suddenly I knew these were not my tears, but His. Not only was He aware of my dilemma, but He was hurting with me too. These drops were His tears. He was crying with me, and for me. One of His children was hurting.

I felt the love of God entering that car with each drop of rain that hit the window. I began to see the love of Jesus flow from Agnes and Margaret. He hadn't left me alone. He had always been there. His presence had been within Gary, Phyllis, Carol, and even my doctors. It was I who hadn't taken the time before this to recognize the love of Jesus within the Christians around me.

The trip to Wichita seemed endless. It was impossible for me to move around to even find a comfortable position. Before we left Dodge City, the nurse had put my winter robe on me. I was hot and restless. Each time I attempted to move, Agnes and Margaret seemed to become more alarmed. I could see the frustration on their faces growing as they tried to figure out how to make me more comfortable. At a highway construction site outside of Wichita, they were required to stop. This caused them to exchange their frustration for good old-fashioned panic.

When we arrived at Wesley Hospital in Wichita, my mom and older sister Kay were anxiously waiting for us. My mother watched as a distraught woman ran into the emergency room demanding a wheelchair immediately. Mom wondered what the emergency was.

As they pulled me from the car, she didn't even recognize me at first. I slumped listless in the chair. She stiffened with disbelief.

I didn't have to wait, but was immediately put into a room. The bed was a needed relief after our long trip. It had been a hard journey on both me and the ladies from Dodge City. They quickly made their exit, exhausted and relieved their good deed had ended. As they left, feeling they had done all they could and knowing they were leaving me in good hands, Margaret couldn't help noticing the shock on my mom's face.

Agnes and Margaret's documented report of our trip to Wichita: Agnes began, "The telephone had rung an

44

hour and a half earlier. It had been Earliene Conrady, our church secretary, inquiring as to whether or not I might be able to drive Sue Winget, our pastor's wife, to the hospital in Wichita. I was sorry to hear that she needed further treatment than could be offered at the Dodge City Hospital, but was delighted that I had been given the opportunity to be a bit of service.

"I had immediately called my dear friend, Margaret Marshall, and she had volunteered to accompany me to Wichita. Beyond that, her husband, Louie, suggested that we take the Marshall automobile since it was larger than mine and was a four-door model.

"Now I stood in the hall of the Dodge City Hospital with my back against a south wall. Only moments earlier I had been greeted by another special friend, Carol Kirchmer, who was attempting to feed Sue her lunch. Carol and I had many experiences together, but never had I seen her face etched with so much anguish. My first glimpse of Sue struck me like a thunderbolt! Carol and I uttered no sounds but our glances toward each other betrayed our many emotions.

"As I stood there, it seemed all I could say, half in a whisper and half to myself, was, 'Dear God... Dear God...!'

"You see, I had known Sue even before the family had moved from Wellsville, Kansas, to Dodge City. Sue had been a vivacious woman who had served our Central Region (American Baptist churches in Kansas and part of Oklahoma) as Fellowship Guild Counselor. Fellowship Guild is an organization for girls within American Baptist churches. Only a few summers earlier, Sue and her daughter, Shannon, had come to attend one of our guild gatherings at Camp Christy near Scott City, Kansas. Perhaps one of my most vivid remembrances of the event had been as Sue stood at the break of day on the peak of a hill, and related to the girls and counselors how she, too, had sometimes been unsure of herself as a young girl growing into adulthood. This had been a real point of identification for the girls. On their faces, you could see these questions: You mean she had problems just like we do now? You mean Jesus Christ can take care of my concerns just like He did hers?

"As I moved back into the hospital room and looked at Sue, I could scarcely believe that the Sue I saw now was the confident, capable, poised young woman I had known earlier. She half sat on the hospital bed unable to focus upon Margaret or me, unable to give a handshake or an embrace, unable to eat or swallow properly, unable to speak fluently.

"Somehow God enabled us to move through the following minutes, and we were now leaving the Dodge City facility to assist Sue in getting into the Marshall vehicle so that we might proceed to Wichita. How grateful I was for the two back doors of the automobile. At best, it was most difficult to assist Sue in any kind of movement. Her limbs were so heavy and practically useless for any kind of voluntary movement. I could not see how she could possibly be comfortable in such a position in the back seat—Wichita was one hundred fifty miles away!

"Just as the car was ready to leave, Gary, her devoted husband, and the children, Shawn, Shannon, and Jason, arrived. Gary was involved with a funeral service and burial and would go to Wichita as soon as he had finished the duties God had given him for that day. Gary's face mirrored such suffering—suffering that perhaps can be seen better by someone who has lost her dearest companion. I was in that category. The faces of Shawn, Shannon , and Jason each in their own way revealed deep questioning fears about their mother. The veneer of their masks slipped just a little. I doubt if the battlefield participants show better control. The embraces were touching; I turned aside as if I might intrude upon these intimate family moments. The car started; Sue held a limp right hand to the back window and pointed upward— that faith did something for all of us as the automobile moved toward Wichita!

46

"Margaret and I are the closest of friends. We are able to communicate honestly. We have a sharing relationship which I consider a supreme gift from God. But on that day as we drove eastward, few words were spoken between us. Margaret drove; and as I sat in the passenger's front seat, I almost wished I had something to do with operating the car. Each time I turned toward Sue reclining in the back, I felt such an utter feeling of helplessness. With each inquiry, she always replied that she was all right. One eye was partially closed, and she seemed to move her body only a little. Somehow it seemed to help—at least me—if I could move her leg position, alter her robe, or even touch her body.

"It was a rainy, dreary day. Road construction was going on. I thought the light would never turn green when we were stopped for one-way traffic. We reached the city limits of Wichita, and I was delighted when Margaret asked me to drive. I remember little about the traffic that day. I do recall how grateful I was to see the symbol of hope on the outside of Wesley Medical Center. I remained at the wheel of the car with Sue as Margaret went inside the hospital to find assistance for admitting her. She came back to the car, with a wheelchair, and managed to get Sue inside where Sue's mother and sister were waiting for our arrival."

Margaret added, "This area of the hospital was a busy place, but very soon two ladies approached us. The older one took one look at Sue and walked over to the window where she stood until she could pull herself together. Obviously she had not been prepared for what she saw. It would have been a shock for any mother.

"Sue's sister took it all in stride and went about the task of giving the girl at the desk the information she needed for the records. Meanwhile Agnes was parking the car as Sue, her mother, and I were escorted to a patient room on another floor. When Sue was settled in bed, the only thing left for us to do was to hold her and her family up in prayer. This we did for weeks to come."

CHAPTER 6

Gary's drive to Wichita was a complete blur. He kept going over and over his thoughts, trying to find some logical reason for all that was happening. He questioned if I had suffered a massive stroke. He had so many chances to ask the doctors this, but he was too afraid to find the answer to his suspicions.

The only relief from his intense fear of the unknown was the security of knowing I was in the hands of a big Lord. He was sure the Lord was bigger than any problem with which we would be confronted, but he was badly in need of Heavenly reassurance and comfort. Shawn felt he was experiencing a nightmare. Surely he would soon awake and find his world put back together. Shawn later wrote down the painful feeling and mixed thoughts he was experiencing:

"When you went to the hospital, Mom—
I felt like there was something missing in my life.
There was nobody around.

I was lonely, very worried.
I was in a strange world, nobody to talk to.
I didn't know what to do or say to anybody.
Confused.
Mom, at times I thought you were going to die.
I felt like I lost a best friend."

Gary and Shawn sat quietly as they traveled, sharing only a few words and their tears of disbelief about what was happening. Numbed by the events of the hectic day, Gary found it difficult to realize that my health was continuing to deteriorate.

I was still feeling as though I were making a journey down a long tunnel, feeling death would come at the end of my journey. I questioned why the Lord was allowing my family to be so torn with grief, seeing me this way. Because I was feeling that I might be near the end of my life, I wondered why He wouldn't just take me and end this agony, showing them His mercy.

Death seemed like such blessed relief to me at this point. I couldn't help being surprised at my response, because just the thought of death always before had sent waves of fear through me. The thought hadn't yet entered my mind that I might be facing a life totally dependent upon others to just get me in and out of bed.

Shawn and Gary arrived that evening, mentally and emotionally drained. Gary had prepared himself, knowing that probably the trip to Wichita would be difficult for me. Although he knew my condition could possibly be worse, even he was not prepared to see me slipping away so quickly.

Because of his exhausted condition, Gary found it difficult to think clearly. His mind was confused by the day's events. Though Shawn felt very strongly that he and his dad should spend the night in the hospital, Gary felt I was in good hands there. He would be in better condition to face Thursday if he had a good night's rest.

He pointed out where the call button was, so I

could get help if I needed it in the night, but I couldn't see the button! After trying every way possible to get me to understand and see the lighted button, he gave up. He called the nurse and she gave me a hand-held button.

No one knew what I was thinking or feeling inside, and I had no way of letting anyone know. Maybe this feeling of traveling down a hall was not a journey towards death as I thought, but each moment that passed seemed to be taking me farther and farther from the life I knew. Maybe this journey was leading me to a life as an invalid and, even worse, to be a prisoner locked up in a body that couldn't see or hear or even react to the world around it.

I was frightened, not just by what was happening, but for where it might lead. As Gary and Shawn were leaving the hospital, I felt so alone, so isolated, so lost. Tears began to fill my eyes, and the thought of never seeing or being with them again began to fill my mind.

For the first time, Gary too, wondered if I would live through the night. Suddenly the assurance that everything would be all right left him.

Somehow the Lord always works it out to give us the support of fellow Christians to strengthen us in our weakness and pick us up when we are down from the weight of life's burdens. The Lord had picked such a roommate for me that night, Peggy Smith.

I couldn't see what she looked like, or even hear her voice. Peggy convinced and assured Gary that although she didn't have the use of her leg because she had M.S., she knew where her call button was, and if necessary she would yell for help. The night before, her roommate had died, and she certainly wanted to do anything within her power to prevent this from happening again.

Slowly Gary dragged himself, exhausted, from the room, with no more to give anyone, but very fearful of what the night would bring. I wanted to scream after him to stop! "Please, don't leave me!" The words rang in my head, unable to be heard by anyone but me. The words wouldn't come. Tears trickled down my cheeks as I lay trapped within my world.

Soon after Gary left me, I was taken down for another x-ray, which left me even more disoriented and confused. After they returned me to my bed, I couldn't find the call button they had given me earlier. I felt totally isolated, unable to call for help. Somewhere I knew Peggy was out there, but how could I let her know I needed her?

I lay there, afraid to close my eyes, fearing that sleep might bring the death which I felt was choking the remaining life out of me. My roommate, Peggy, too, was afraid to sleep. She kept an agonized, prayerful watch throughout the night.

With morning, I strained to make some visible sense of the shadows I could see in the dense fog through which I was looking. I was aware there was something on the wall, but I wasn't sure just what it was. As I strained to see what was there, I began to see the outlines of two blurred crosses. I wondered why they would hang them so close together at such a weird angle.

As my mind became clearer, I realized there was only one cross, and that I was seeing double. Even though I was seeing double, I rejoiced, feeling surely this was an improvement. At least I could see. I couldn't keep my eyes off that cross, even if I was seeing two of it. It seemed to bring me such inner peace. I could sense the presence of the Lord in that room through my cross. Suddenly, too, I was very much aware of the fact that I was still alive.

The night had proved to be difficult for both Peggy and me. Her watch was more exhausting than she could physically handle, and my body was stiff from not being able to move in bed.

In the morning, Gary and my mom arrived at the hospital early, hoping to see the doctor and find needed answers to our grave situation. Realizing the night had been difficult for both Peggy and me, Gary decided to stay at night from then on. Arrangements were made to put me in a private room, which relieved Peggy of her willing, but unneeded, burden.

The doctor prepared us for a day of tests, and no answers. Another brain scan was to be taken, along with a brain wave, an evoked-response test. He warned that a spinal tap was needed within a few days.

Upon examination, he found my left eye to be unresponsive. It seemed paralyzed as he touched it with a tissue. He held a tuning fork near my ear and I heard nothing. My speech was slurred and not understandable.

My arms and legs flailed as though they were directed by someone else's body. My face was sagging around the left side of my mouth, causing me to feel as though I were drooling.

They wheeled my gurney from one test to another. I was becoming more and more anxious as the day progressed. I didn't want Gary to leave my side. The frustration was building in me as the technicians gave me instructions I could neither hear nor understand as they performed the necessary tests. I wanted so badly to be helpful, but I just couldn't seem to make my body do what they asked.

Everything was going so fast, I couldn't cope with it. Gary somehow could see the frustration building, and he kept trying to reassure me and promised not to leave me.

The day for him, and the rest of my family, too, was a day of anxiety and uncertainty as they all waited fearfully, afraid of what might be found. They were forced to stand helplessly by and continue to watch me drifting away.

By evening, most of my family had gathered. There was a lobby down the hall from my room that was becoming increasingly filled by my clan. My father, brother, and two brothers-in-law had joined my mother, three sisters, and Gary and Shawn in the wait.

I was flooded and supported by the love of this wonderful family. I was feeling so much love for each one of them flowing, almost bubbling out of me, and I just wished they could each feel it.

Even though distance keeps my family apart much of the time, when we need each other we band together. It was true this time. I was hoping, if the future gave me a chance, I too, would do the same thing.

Because I was becoming more restless from my long day of tests, visitors were limited. Already someone was there from Dodge City to check on my condition— Virginia Smith, a school teacher taking summer courses in Wichita . There were also several ministers who had known Gary.

One minister and his wife were Hal and Linda Hale. Hal had been one of our assistant ministers at Wellsville Baptist Church. They now were serving a church in Wichita. During their stay at Wellsville, they had become extremely dear friends. Linda was grieved by the condition in which she found me when she arrived at the hospital:

"I had been praying throughout the day, claiming a portion of Scripture from the Book of Hebrews that God had laid on my heart for someone, I wasn't sure who. I didn't know until later that day that it was for Sue!

"Gary phoned me that morning to tell me Sue was in the hospital; he told me to be prepared. Sue couldn't see or hear and she had no muscle control.

"I tried to conjure a mental picture of what Sue might look like, and yet found myself totally unprepared for the reality of her condition.

"Sue was pale and seemed very frightened and disoriented. It was obvious that she was looking right at you, but not seeing you. She tried several times to say something, but her speech was very garbled; I couldn't understand her!

"When she tried to convey a message to us we couldn't interpret, she became extremely frustrated, crying easily. Even her crying sounded grossly distorted.

"Once when she'd been crying a tissue was placed

in her hand, to wipe her nose. It was a great effort for her even get the tissue to her nose. Her efforts appeared to look much like those of a quadriplegic.

"It was very disturbing to see Sue totally incapacitated. It was hard to believe that such a drastic change could take place, so quickly.

"Hal and I didn't stay long; she was obviously in no condition for visitors. I leaned over her and shared the Scripture I'd been claiming all day. As I read the passage, we both cried. I had a very real sense that Sue was going to die.

"On our way home Hal said to me, 'I don't think Sue's gonna make it.' I shared with him the feeling I had experienced, as I read to her from my Bible.

"When we got home we went before the Lord, asking for His healing for Sue."

Going to the bathroom was a major problem. Because I was like dead weight, Gary would stand me up, set me on a portable commode and lay my head on his shoulder. I was unable to even hold my head up.

Friday, the doctor reported there was a difference between the brain scans taken in Dodge City and those in Wichita. The new scan had shown increased swelling on the left side of my brain. This would explain the deterioration in my condition. Even though the other test hadn't come back, and wouldn't be back until after the weekend, he thought it best to begin treatment for multiple sclerosis. He wasn't sure if that was what we were going to find, because M.S. was usually a slow-moving disease, which didn't strike this quickly , or this severely.

Since my condition was still seeming to worsen, he said we had nothing to lose, only to gain. If I did have M.S., I should respond to the A.C.T.H. within three days, before any change would be noticed. This could possibly give them still more proof of what was causing the problem. Everyone was relieved that at least something would be done, right or wrong.

To Gary and me, the thought I might have M.S. seemed easy to accept at this moment, although I'm sure we wouldn't have been able to just a few short days before. There were many diagnoses that frightened us more now, and M.S. seemed the least of several evils, although we had to admit we knew little about the disease. My mom, however, was still not ready to accept it, and wouldn't, she announced, until she had to do so.

The A.C.T.H. was to be given to me in eight hour IV's, once a day, for fourteen days. A heparin lock was put into my arm, in the hope that a new IV wouldn't need to be started every day. Because the A.C.T.H. was such strong medication, it irritated the veins quickly, and would cause them to become easily inflamed.

Even though I didn't have much feeling in my arms, I felt the irritation of the IVs as the medication entered my arm. I knew it was the price I must pay, and a small one, if I intended to get well.

CHAPTER 7

Since the onset of this attack several days earlier, I had a strong inner feeling. Sometimes this inner knowing even seemed to be an audible, reassuring voice which could be heard only in my head. I began to believe this promise—and hung onto it, knowing it had to be coming from the Lord—a promise that I was going to have a miracle. My miracle was going to be slow. How long it was going to take I didn't know, but my miracle was all I had to cling to. My constant prayer became, "Lord, you have given me an opportunity to prove that my faith in You is real. Please don't let this be happening to me for no reason. Let me learn what You want me to learn." Right at this point in my life, I was a complete invalid, totally dependent upon those around me to meet my every need. Even though it looked like medically I might spend the rest of my life in this condition, I began claiming the promise that I was going to have a miracle in my life. I also knew, from my inner source, that this miracle was going to come through a gradual process, over a period of time. I somehow knew just lying around waiting for my miracle to happen wasn't what the Lord intended, and it wasn't something I had to earn either; it was to be a gift. He would give me His best, and I knew He would give me the strength to do my best for Him. I tried to second-guess the Lord, trying to figure out how long it would take before I would be up and going.

I am the type of person who wants to learn and grow from my experiences in life, and this was no exception. I believe the verse in the Bible that says:

"And we know that all that happens to us is working for our good if we love God and are fitting into his plans" (Romans 8:28) (TLB).

If this is true, and I believe it is, the Lord can use each circumstance that invades our lives to teach us something, and I wasn't about to go through all of this without learning anything the Lord could teach me. However, I must admit it was easier to learn from the Lord Himself what He wanted me to know than to learn what other well-meaning supporters thought I needed to know at this critical point in my life.

They had no way of knowing exactly what I was going through nor how I was really feeling. Sermons and sermonettes from those who felt they had all the answers to life's struggles and pain were not easy to digest at this time in my life. I was badly in need of sustaining love. I was in the worst storm of my life. I was not needing someone to throw me an anchor, to ensure my sinking, but rather a buoy to hold me up until the storm was over.

How many times, I thought back, had I been there when someone was hurting from one of life's low blows, just to offer what I felt were necessary words of wisdom? Maybe my seemingly brilliant words of encouragement had stung an already-gaping wound in the person who in fact turned out to be my victim. Perhaps all that was needed, and all I wanted now, was a hug of encouragement, and the love and support of a friend.

The next thirty-six hours were spent waiting to see just how, or if, I would respond to the medication. With the start of the A.C.T.H., my condition ceased to deteriorate, and leveled off. By the end of the first day, I wasn't improving, but I wasn't getting any worse.

Gary was finally able by late Friday to get in touch with our adopted twenty-year-old daughter, Pam Reeves, living in Salina, Kansas.

We had gotten our Pam as a foster child when she was fourteen-years old. At that time, she had been an abused child, filled with distrust and anger. She tested our love with every action. We had cared for over twenty foster children when we lived in Wellsville. Each one will always hold a special place in our hearts, but there was something extra-special about Pam. Though she went home once, she asked to come back—this time, not as our foster child, but as our daughter. Though legally still a "Reeves" by name, in her heart, where it really counts, she is a "Winget" to the core.

Pam could hardly wait until Saturday to check on her "Mom Sue," wondering if she would lose the only mom who didn't always agree with her, but whom she knew always loved her.

Saturday morning the doctor decided he wasn't going to wait until after the weekend to do the spinal tap, but do it now. How I was dreading that test! I think it was just all the stories I had heard on the subject that worried me. When he entered the room with that long needle, even I could see it.

I decided I had a lot to be thankful for; after all, he hadn't given me time to worry, and I didn't have to think about it all weekend. Since I was numb almost all over, I didn't feel it that much anyway. My worrying took more out of me than the spinal tap.

Since I couldn't sit up for the test, he had to do it in a different location than usual along the spine, and I would have to lie still for six hours. It was decided by my father that my unregistered nurses, consisting of my two sisters and my mom, would be banned from the room during the six hours. My dad would stay with me. Usually a quiet man, he would find it easier to keep me quiet, he felt. My mom and sisters all suffer from an over-active crazy bone, making lying still really impossible.

The first night I was in the hospital at Wichita, my mom decided there had been enough tears. Humor and laughter had become a necessary part of our survival, and my recovery. Passing by in the hall, one might think we were having a wild party, instead of fighting for a life. Tears did come, but masked behind laughter.

One of the first nights I was in the hospital, my sister Debi asked me if I wanted a milkshake. I responded with a positive shake of my head. The problem then became trying to understand what flavor I wanted. Because Debi has a deaf son, she was finally able to understand my drawn-out, labored speech—all too familiar to her. She then phoned her husband to fill my order. She told him to get a butterscotch shake, but she said it just as I had, drawing out each syllable.

His response was shock, and he replied back that he didn't know where he could even get a "Bud" or a "Scotch" milkshake, and he wasn't sure if they even made such a thing.

He was thinking, "She must really be bad if she's going to take up drinking now!" Momentarily the silence and tranquility of the hospital were broken by rolls of uncontrolled laughter.

Rod was not the only one who brought a needed break in the tension. Mom and Kay's nursing knowledge and skill also brought many an "unhospital-like" response.

For instance, during my six-hour wait flat in bed following the spinal tap, I really had worked my bladder overtime. Trying to use the bed pan when lying flat on one's back not only is a difficult transaction under the best of conditions, but tends to put one in an awkward, uphill, head-down position to obtain relief. Anyway, it was asking too much of me to succeed at this seemingly dangerous and difficult feat. Waiting the six hours was not an easy task, either.

When I could finally get out of bed to use the portable commode, Kay quickly grabbed what looked to her like the right pan and inserted it under the lid. Much to her shock and surprise, I filled it to the rim. Uncertain how to best empty it, they left it there. When Gary arrived from the motel, after a much-needed nap, he could tell immediately they had used my wash pan instead of the right one! Since the pan was held in by a spring, his job was not easy. He was the only person in the room not laughing.

For a day or two, the medication just retarded the deterioration of my health. By Sunday, the thirty-six hour period of waiting had ended. The weekend had been spent waiting, not only by those assembed, but by those who waited for hourly and daily reports, in Dodge City, Wellsville, and throughout Kansas, even as far away as Pennsylvania.

Gary and I, as well as my family, were literally carried through this time of need by the overwhelming prayer support. I know Heaven's switch-board was jammed. My condition couldn't help improving. By Sunday we could all tell that, in fact, it was improving. Not only had the deterioration stopped, but my speech was beginning to sound more comprehensible.

I was beginning to look toward all the work that lay ahead of me, instead of watching my life drift into the unknown. The gloom that had hung heavily over us all was replaced with a bright ray of hope and new joy.

Everyone realized that as a family, we had a battle ahead of us to fight. Debi thought my room needed a little cheering up. She brought in a poster that was to be an inspiration and a challenge to us all. On it was a majestic sunrise. In its shadow were two mountain climbers attempting to climb their mountain. Inscribed on it were the challenging words:

> "Praise God!
> He gives us mountains to climb...
> and strength to climb them."

Debi taped this on my wall, along with pictures of my three children climbing the mountain with me.

God surely had given us a mountain to climb. They all heartily, supportingly, let me know this was a mountain we would be climbing together. I would not have to climb it alone.

On the wall next to my poster were hung all the cards and letters that came in from supporting friends. This became our shared wall. Each card that was placed on the wall became a reminder that the sender too was joining our battle and helping us climb our mountain. The cards hung there, reminding us that not only did we have the strength and guidance of a God worthy to be praised; but in our hour of need, He was providing us with this extra boost of support from friends, family, and even people we didn't know. Not only the cards reminded us of all our supporters, the scent and beauty of over twenty plants and flowers filled the room with love. I could smell the fragrance and I felt strongly the support of the senders. I longed for the day that I could see their beauty clearly.

The phone was continually ringing with very welcome words from those seeking current information. This provided strength to our growing army, fighting in our battle, and joining the climb up our steep mountain.

Sunday, even though I was showing some improvement, all my joints were aching and becoming stiff. I didn't care at this point: I was alive! Just the joy of that would carry me through until Tuesday when Dr. Barnett would come in with all the test results, and a possible diagnosis.

Tuesday morning, Dr. Barnett entered looking very somber. He promptly asked everyone to leave but Gary and me. I could see the terrified looks in my family as they slowly filed from the room. I could tell by the stern look deep within the doctor's eyes that the news was not good. I began to quickly prepare myself for this news, whatever it was to be.

Dr. Barnett was a sober, quiet-spoken man, who took his work very seriously. We hadn't seen him smile once since I had been in the hospital. Today he looked more unsmiling than usual. He was a man who dealt with so much sadness, as a neurologist.

He began to talk slowly, so softly that I was unable to catch every word. He began to relate the test results and his findings during the physical examination. Though he was only 90% sure, all the tests supported his diagnosis of multiple sclerosis.

Not having any knowledge of the disease, I asked him if my case was severe. He responded, "Your attack was very severe—one of the fastest I've seen." He had not seen M.S. come in the form of a sudden attack. It's a slow, progressive, deteriorating disease.

He explained that in M.S. the spinal cord is much like an electrical cord that has "shorted out" because the rubber has been worn off in places. Similarly the M.S. attacks the nerves on the spinal cord, causing them to "short out," or malfunction. The spinal cord might then try to patch itself, often causing scar tissue. This would then affect a message sent from the brain, through the spine, to the body. The scar tissue could cause the body not to receive a message sent to it, or perhaps misinterpret the message.

This explained why I could think of a word, knowing exactly what I intended to say, and yet open my mouth, much to my surprise, and hear another word jump out. This had been making communication extremely frus-

62

trating for me and those struggling to understand me as well.

Dr. Barnett further explained that in his opinion there were three things that were important: first, the medication A.C.T.H.; second, physical therapy; and third, most important of all, a positive attitude. Being positive, he assured me, would make my battle halfway won already.

After he delivered his news and answered our many questions, he quickly left the room. We had finally found an answer. We knew for the first time who or what we were fighting. A sense of relief filled my room. We could begin our battle, knowing what this enemy's name was. We were going to fight, and beat, this enemy.

In my mind, I knew the doctor was only partly right. Instead of just the three ingredients he said I needed to fight this battle, I needed four. The first point of my battle strategy would have to be to trust in the Lord. Was my faith strong enough?

During the days I had hung so close to death, there had been plenty of time to reflect upon my life. I knew my life hadn't been lived dedicated to the Lord in the last few years. The thought of coming face to face with the God who had made me, knowing He would be disappointed with the path that I had freely chosen to follow to live out my life, deeply shamed and grieved me.

Now, when I had nowhere to look but up to Him, He was there waiting patiently, as always before to offer His always unearned, overflowing grace and mercy.

The doctor had just made his exit when my entire family, waiting anxiously outside the door, fell into the room, hopeful for some answers.

Unable to wait a moment longer, Mom questioned us, "What did he say?"

Not knowing how she would receive our news, I slowly answered the question she had waited over a year to be answered, "He said he's ninety percent sure I have M.S."

Suddenly her past fears became a reality. Over the past months she had refused to accept any possible grave diagnosis. She looked at me and said, "Does that mean I have to accept it now?"

"Yes," I said, "at least we know who the enemy is. Now we start fighting."

We all sat staring off into space, though prewarned of the possible news, but still needing time for everyone to process in his mind this new name that had intruded into our lives: multiple sclerosis.

CHAPTER 8

The doctor ordered a patch put over one eye, to be
alternated daily. He was certain this would help my
double vision.

As I lay in my hospital bed trying to absorb this
new name that was changing our lives, I couldn't help
thinking about the people in our Dodge City church. How
would they respond to the news of my illness? I hadn't
known I had M.S. when they called us to their church.
Would they regret their decision now? I remembered the
night we had been asked to come to the First Baptist
Church of Dodge City to decide if Gary was to be their new
minister.

The pastor's office had seemed so cold and dark.
The walls were covered with a dark brown, almost black,
paneling. Covering one wall was a huge empty bookshelf,
waiting to be filled by the one chosen to be the pastor of
the church of Dodge City. This was the reason the office

looked so lifeless, almost frighteningly cold. At least it looked that way to me that day at the end of January 1984. Not only was it cold outside in that western Kansas town, but I was cold deep inside myself, and tension and fear gripped me and my entire family as we waited for that knock on the door.

I was constantly questioning why we were there, not only in that cold, lifeless office, but why we were even considering a move to a distant, seemingly far-off city. Gary had just candidated to be their new pastor.

The church had chosen a pulpit committee; in this church it consisted of twenty-five members, an unusually large number. The Pulpit Committee was chosen from their Deacons, Trustees, Board of Education, and men, women, and youth organizations. They visited different churches searching for a new minister. We had been talking with the committee for almost six months before we had been asked to come and candidate. Gary was to speak in the pulpit Sunday morning, followed by a reception for us. He was also to speak Sunday night, and then the church was to vote as to whether they wanted him as their new pastor. We would then give them our answer.

Though the vote was to decide if they wanted Gary as their pastor, all five of us knew our lives could be changed by the outcome. This situation had seemed so right for Gary. The oppportunities of this pastorate really excited and challenged him, but now we had to wait for the outcome of the church vote. Not only was the tension of waiting weighing heavily upon me, but I also wondered what our response to the vote would be.

I questioned deep within myself why we would even consider such a move. Weren't we so happy and content in our present church home in Wellsville, Kansas? I wondered if that was why we were being challenged by the Lord. Were we too secure—too content? It is so easy to depend on one's self, instead of the Lord, when one's life is so easy to control and so dependable. This new situation would mean challenges and opportunities for all of us in my family. It would challenge not only our lives, but challenge each one of us in our relationship to our Lord. I could see the advantage for each member of my family, but I couldn't help wondering, "What about me?" I fought feelings of self-pity and shame as I sat and waited for my life to be decided. My feelings felt like a yo-yo; if, in fact, it was the will of the Lord, why would He want us to leave the security and love of the Wellsville church? What did He have planned for me? At the present time, if we moved, I would have to give up my dream of earning a Master's Degree. This was a goal I had been working on for several years. Would this be something He was asking me to give up, for the present time anyway? This wasn't the first time I had to discontinue my work on a degree. It deeply hurt to think the Lord was going to ask me to give up my goal yet again. It seemed that if we made this move, there were several goals I would have to give up.

I was fighting my feelings and fears, also concerned that the people upstairs might be unaware of my problems with unstable health. Would that situation make a difference as they voted?

I had been having a problem with my lungs for over a year. I had continual lung infections. The doctor in Wellsville felt I possibly had Lupus Erythematosus. This was a long name that I knew little about, and I was also very hesitant even to talk about the subject. I suppose this was because the more I talked about Lupus, the more real the possibility became that I might have the disease.

We had gone through a difficult year trying to get a definite diagnosis. Thousands of dollars and several puzzled doctors later left us with the knowledge that my lungs were not draining properly. Although I had been placed in the hospital for nearly a month, where an endless group of tests were done, all came to a dead end. I was frustrated with doctors, as I'm sure they were frustrated with me. Somehow I was not fitting into their textbook diagnoses.

I kept crying out to the Lord for an answer. I felt

like He wouldn't hear or couldn't hear my pleading and prayers, or that He was playing one big joke at my expense. My faith in my doctors was greater than in my God. The doctors had let me down, so I felt my God had let me down, too. I felt very much alone in my fight against my illness: I was fighting an enemy I didn't even know.

Because of my frustration, I began putting my trust in others' faith, not even able to trust in my own faith. I felt very much out of step with the Lord, and hoped those around me might somehow get through to Him on their prayer channel.

I began a fight against the unknown illness, not totally convinced I was battling Lupus. I had been told that it could take possibly five years to confirm this diagnosis. Besides, I couldn't believe anything serious would happen to me.

I knew the Lord could heal me, if it were His will. The Lord and I hadn't exactly been on speaking terms lately. Gary had told me many times that I didn't like it when things were not done my way. Of course, this was just one man's opinion, but maybe the Lord's observation, too. My feeling at this point was that I would just have to learn to live with my lung trouble, no matter what it was.

I felt I had everything under control. In the past months I had started doing a lot of walking. It appeared that my health problems were a part of my past, too insignificant even to be brought up when we were candidating. I sat and pondered upon this as we waited for the results of the vote. I wondered if it would make a difference if these people knew. After all, wouldn't they want a healthy pastor's wife? I wasn't sure they would consider me a "normal - healthy" person. I wondered if I would qualify in this position. I was afraid that my health situation might prohibit Gary from becoming the pastor of the church he had dreamed of having.

For a few minutes, I forgot the decision was to be made by the Lord and not by my limitations.

As we waited for the answer to the vote, I questioned what our reply would be. As my mind jumped from one question to another I sat rigid in my chair, unable to find an answer.

My heart beat quickened when there was finally a knock on the door. It had seemed such a long wait. Our future would possibly be determined by the news, good or bad, waiting on the other side of that door. Mike Havercroft entered the room. He said excitedly, "The church voted for you to come be our new pastor! We've made our decision; now it's up to you!" Seeing the puzzled look on our faces, he turned to leave, saying, "I'll give you some time alone as a family." He shut the door as he left.

Gary turned to the family and asked for a vote. Not really knowing all that this decision involved, all the hands of the children went up excitedly.

Gary left the room to tell Mike, who was anxiously waiting, that we would accept the call. I had been unable to raise my hand when Gary had asked for the family vote. In his excitement, he hadn't even noticed my last-minute hesitation. At this moment, my feelings were so confused. Part of me knew it was the Lord's will, but part of me began to grieve immediately over the death of our eight-year-old ministry in Wellsville.

Crying never seemed to be something that was a part of me. If I cried once a year it was unusual, and I didn't cry in front of people I didn't know. But now my eyes began to fill with tears, and before I was even aware of it, I was crying unashamedly. It could have been caused by all the tension of nearly six months of negotiation with the pulpit committee, or it could have just been the reality of leaving Wellsville; I didn't know for sure.

My response puzzled those waiting outside the office to greet their new pastor.

I continued to cry as we were welcomed with many hugs from our new church family. The progression of hugs led to Carol Kirchmer. I found myself sobbing freely in her understanding arms. As she held me she turned to Gary, saying "You be good to her this month." Gary nodded in agreement.

We had a month to move from Wellsville to Dodge City. In eight years one can collect an awful lot of junk, as well as treasures. Many times these treasures have to be stored and moved from a location locked within our hearts. I was questioning whether our three children were really aware of the fact we were not moving all the city of Wellsville to Dodge City with us when we moved.

I was fairly certain Shawn, our thirteen-year-old, knew this. He had had to adjust to moving before. However, since Shannon, our ten-year-old daughter, and Jason, our nine-year-old, had joined our clan, they hadn't known any other existence except our life in Wellsville, Kansas. I feared they didn't know what lay ahead in leaving their friends, nor what to expect in the months ahead of them in a new location. Time was to prove my suspicions. Not only were they not prepared for the often rough road, but neither was I. Saying farewell to friends in Wellsville and to the Wellsville Baptist Church was difficult for all of us. Our roots were deeper than any of us knew. Our lives had been so full and secure while we lived there. Each of us in his own way had felt so loved by these people, not only within the church, but in the community as well. The time had come for us to leave that extremely close small community and the security it offered. Tearfully trusting the Lord, we packed our van to the ceiling with my special possessions and crammed the car with our most treasured creatures, Shawn, Shannon, Jason, and the family part-poodle, part brown dog , Heidi. On March 9th, 1984, we ended one chapter of our lives and began another .

We felt very sure of God's leading to Dodge City. Any doubts, at least within Gary and me, were quickly erased. Almost immediately we felt the warmth from the people. However, this did not diminish the difficulties in adjusting, especially for Shannon and Jason. They found it difficult to make new friends and adjust to their new school. Almost daily I was faced with tears as they entered the house from school. Shawn's adjustment came almost immediately because of his interest and participation in athletics.

For Gary, the move was the easiest. He had grown up only forty miles from Dodge City , where his parents were still living. I was from Eastern Kansas, and made several Western Kansas cultural errors that quickly gave me away as a city girl. It wasn't difficult for anyone with any knowledge on the subject of farming to discover I knew nothing about cattle. Once, after hearing an announcement on the T.V. I innocently asked, "Who is Mr. Stockmen?"

After gaining control of herself from her laughter, Phyllis answered, "There is no Mr. Stockmen. It is a stockmen's advisory, which means to bring in your cattle from the fields because the weather is going to get bad." I was adapting rather quickly. I learned to ask Gary any questions I might have; and then only in our bedroom with the door shut.

After a month, the strain of the move was beginning to take its toll on me physically. I just blamed the fatigue, occasional faintness, and aching joints on all the stress we had been under.

The reality that something was seriously wrong with me never even entered my mind. Norma Jarett, a registered nurse in our church, urged me with concern, "Sue, you really need to see a specialist. There must be something wrong."

"Norma, it's no use! I've already seen at least five different doctors." She continued her urging for nearly an hour. I was surprised by her concern since she had known me such a short time. Even with constant urging, I wouldn't consent to going to yet another new doctor. It seemed so futile.

My life was too fulfilled to spend any time or energy on my health. I knew time and rest would take care of the problems. Everything else seemed to be going along just great. Not only was Gary serving a larger church, but we had a beautiful parsonage, three beautiful, healthy children, and a super marriage. Even my singing ministry seemed to be budding. In the weeks prior to Mother's Day I was speaking and singing at five Mother and Daughter Banquets. I felt satisfied as my daughter Shannon and I performed, driving over nine hundred miles as we shared and sang together.

Now as I looked back on that portion of my life, I wondered what would have happened if I had listened to Norma? My mind always came back to the same question: How would the people in Dodge City react to an invalid as the wife of their minister? The answer to this question began to haunt me.

Oh, why hadn't the Lord left us in Wellsville?

CHAPTER 9

    I was to have therapy three times a day, which—
with all my visitors —I found damaging to my social
calendar. I had two daily sessions of physical therapy,
and one session of occupational therapy. It made my day
very exhausting, and drained me of what little energy I
did have.

    The noise in physical therapy made it difficult for
me to follow direction, and the simplest movement was
hard work. The physical therapy room at Wesley hospital
was a large open room. As one entered the room, on the far
left was a smaller room where the whirlpool therapy was
done. The roar of the machines was deafening to me.
There also were people all around me, evidently talking to
me. I wasn't sure, because I couldn't hear what they were
saying. All I knew was that I was surrounded by grief and
sadness. I could hear their cries and groanings, but I was

unable to see their distress.

My mom always went with me to therapy sessions; I tried to view the world around me through her eyes as she described what she was seeing.

"Oh, Sue," she shared, "there is an elderly woman. She seems to be in so much pain!" Mom slowly walked over to the woman and began talking to her, openly showing her concern.

When she returned, I quickly asked , "What happened?"

I could sense the concern in Mom's voice as she reported, "She fell and broke her hip. There's Peggy," she added. "Remember, she was your roommate the first night you were here?" She buzzed off once again to talk with Peggy.

"I feel a close bond to Peggy and yet I've never seen her or even heard her voice," I thought.

Mom took the time we were in physical therapy to give her love to many of the hurting patients that she saw daily. It helped to relieve her intense pain to extend herself to others with needs.

There were many strange situations to see in therapy, if one could see. I'm sure I was one of these strange sights. One day as I was sitting in my wheel chair waiting for my session to begin, Mom began to laugh.

I asked, " What are you laughing at?"

So I could hear her, she bent down very close to my ear and responded, " There is a retarded girl about twenty years old here for therapy with a broken foot. She said when she saw your patched eye, 'Oh, poor thing, she broke her eye!'"

Though it was difficult for my mom to accept the diagnosis of multiple sclerosis, she had a strong spirit and she believed with Gary and me that we had to have a miracle. She would do all within her power, even if she had to knock a few gates down in Heaven, to get one. Combined with a hug and kiss, Mom constantly gave me the necessary encouragement I needed to continue my climb to recovery.

Nights were long and lonely, so Gary felt it was necessary to be with me to help eliminate my distress as well as his. It was reassuring to have him close to me. He was feeling the responsibilities of his new job in Dodge City, though the church tried to assure him his job at present was with me. For his own peace of mind, he thought it necessary to go back to Dodge City for at least some services.

He was trying to rest most days, though he often found it difficult, because I demanded he be near me most of the time. My parents would stay during the days so he could try to get some rest. He was feeling very torn trying to please everyone, all the time wondering if he were going to have to quit his job at the church, just to take care of me.

Jean Stephenson, my therapist, stopped in the middle of one of our sessions: turning to me she said, "Sue, all of us here in therapy are worried that you aren't adjusting to your illness. Just a few days ago you appeared normal. This illness has happened so quickly and so severely. Since you have been here in the hospital you have been surrounded with company. I'm afraid you haven't had a chance to adjust." She questioned whether I actually had accepted my sudden disability, with all the people around me to keep my mind occupied. She questioned , "What will happen when you don't have all the support?"

It gave me a chance to share what a great God I had and what I believed He was going to do for me. I told her of the early morning sessions I held with just myself, long before Gary awakened. Though not a time I looked forward to, it was a time when the tears flowed freely, and my thoughts ran wild. It was a time when I freely grieved, fearing the "Sue" that I had been and known was gone forever. This new person taking over her body was so foreign to me. To my suprise I found that I missed the old "Sue," and longed for her to come back.

Following my morning therapy sessions, Mom and

I were always greeted with welcome letters and cards filled with prayer support from friends wishing us well. We were even hearing from people we didn't know.

We were overwhelmed by the number of churches that had put my name on their prayer chains and prayer lists. The prayers of others had never been so necessary or vital in my life. I felt a strong need for them and I cherished them all. I couldn't believe the Lord had burdened so many to pray for me.

Linda Hale had gone to our regional Women's Conference and reported my circumstances, asking for prayers. Since I was a past officer of the region, many people remembered me. I was flooded with cards and prayers from women throughout the state. They, along with their churches, joined us in our miracle.

I felt a strong need to make frequent calls to Phyllis in Dodge City. Every friendship is unique in its own way, and this relationship was no different. It was based on a dependence growing out of the death of someone I had never had the privilege to meet. My feeling of responsibility was only increased when I had felt so close to actually meeting Bob through experiencing the sensation of imminent death. I had, in my confused state, envisioned him telling me that she needed me, and he was pleased that we were becoming fast friends.

This vision seemed very real to me, burning a conviction deep within my heart. In my present condition I wasn't sure how the Lord was going to fulfill this mission through me, and I wondered if I would ever be needed by anyone again.

It was hard for Phyllis to stay in Dodge City not knowing for sure what was taking place in Wichita. If my mom and sisters hadn't been there already to help care for me, her bags would have been packed and she would have been on her way, but she felt some relief knowing I was in good hands.

Things had been happening so quickly when I was in the Dodge City hospital that there had been no time to get her mixed-up thoughts arranged. She found it very difficult to make any sense out of my illness. Though I usually was the one who was the "deep thinker," her mind was now doing the searching.

"Why did the Lord lead them to Dodge City, just to let me get close to Sue and then take her away?" she questioned. There seemed to be no relief and no easy answers to her questions.

The growing sense of dependence between us was deepening as the threads of our short, intense friendship were being woven tighter and tighter.

She felt it necessary to make the long trip to Wichita. When I asked her to come, her decision was made. She would come. Anxiously, she came to Wichita, hopeful to find me making a fast recovery. Surely, she reasoned, the swelling in my brain would be down by now, and everything would be back to normal.

Though I was improved slightly from when she had last seen me, I wasn't the same Sue she knew. Phyllis could see that this person wasn't the same self-reliant person, but was totally dependent upon others to meet all her needs.

She could sense that I was feeling cut off from my new world back in Dodge City. I was wondering if they would, or could, accept me back there as an invalid. I felt I was no longer a whole person. I hadn't been this way a few short months ago when they had called Gary as their pastor. Would they change their minds and not want him now? Was I going to ruin his ministry there?

Phyllis found it difficult to reassure me. Their acceptance was something I would have to experience for myself, she knew, but she would be there to support me if I needed her.

Betty Wheeler, a member of our church, called Phyllis to check on my condition. In their conversation, Phyllis related my fear of not being accepted by the church people. Dean and Betty, as well as others who heard of my feelings, were distressed about my uncertainty. The

Wheelers made a special trip down to Wichita on the Fourth of July, just to ease my mind. They brought me many personal greetings from Dodge City.

They were deeply troubled when they saw me. They could see how much rehabilitation I needed. As they drove back to Dodge City, Betty said in anguish, "She has so far to come; it will be like physically beginning her life over."

Not knowing I would have company from Dodge City, I had been concerned the holiday would drag, especially because there would be no mail, my link with the world outside the hospital. My parents knew how often the mail kept my spirits up and provided me extra strength. They arranged for a nurse to deliver a card from each of them. Those two cards, one from my dad and one from my mom, became so special, as they too joined the card wall with the many others.

Since I was still in the hopital over the "firecracker" holiday, my parents and Kay were to join Gary, Shawn, and me to watch the fireworks from the window of my room. They moved my bed over to the window, hoping I might be able to enjoy the bursts and brilliant flickering of the fireworks as they exploded on the horizon. Set to music, I'm sure it was a beautiful sight; at least it would be under normal circumstances.

Due to the lateness of the hour, before the spectacle even began I was ready for the finale. The music sounded like jumbled noise in my ears. My legs and feet were cramping, and the fatigue I was fighting seemed to be pulling any available energy that I might have from my body, as though it were being sucked out by some sort of beast. I had been extremely tired in my lifetime, but this was something new.

My days were spent either just lying in bed, or, for a little variety, reclining in the lounge chair. Always I was weighted down with this new fatigue that had somehow found its way into my life. Every move I made had to be fought against this powerful force.

The cramps in my legs and feet were becoming a frequent source of pain and discomfort. They were accompanied by a dull ache deep within my muscles. I wasn't sure if the physical therapy was helping or causing the problem.

I did have to be extremely careful. A broken bone would have difficulty healing while I was on the A.C.T.H. Falling was a real danger in my condition. As careful as my "keepers" were trying to be, I was difficult to manage and I fell several times, luckily never dropping clear to the floor.

Jason and Shannon had spent the first week with Gary's parents in Hanston, Kansas. They were anxious to get to Wichita to see how I was doing, since their last hurried glimpse back in Dodge City. They had been badly frightened by this last encounter. Gary's parents hadn't seen me yet, but they were sure the children were just upset and overstating the seriousness of the condition in which they had seen me.

Shannon, though apprehensive, was considerably relieved. She and Jason were allowed to come up to my room. Although my speech was not a lot better, she reasoned, it had improved, and she was also impressed that I could now hold things in my hands.

Gary, too, had tried to prepare his parents for what they were to see, although he hesitated to paint too black a picture. They were so distressed, fearing I would be a total invalid, and seeing no hope in a situation that bad.

Feeling very much alone and abandoned, Gary felt an inner need to be with all three children to see how they were dealing with our family crisis. He was certain, by now, he wasn't going to lose me to death, but it was difficult to believe I was the wife he had shared so much of himself with. He needed to feel the closeness of our children to try to ease the ache and grief deep inside himself.

My parents' church (where I had spent much of my youth), began putting weekly reports of my condition in their Sunday morning bulletin. Friends I had lost touch with sent loving letters of support. A childhood friend, Joyce Cobb, and her mother, Melba Jacoby, a very close friend of my mother's, both came to Wichita to let us know they were climbing our mountain with us.

My hospital room had ministers from different denominations almost daily, as well as our own. These men each brought comfort in their own way. Even the Methodist minister, from Wellsville, accompanied by one of my "ole walking buddies," his wife Kathy came to see me.

Though my days in the hospital seemed long, they were full and memorable. I felt so much love flying at me from all directions.

It came from the staff there at Wesley, who often dropped by to share in a laugh.

It came from friends who seemed to carry us through visits, flowers, letters, and cards.

It came though the awesome support of my family.

It came pouring out of our three children, often uncertainly, but always there.

It came to me from Gary, unlimited, and unashamed.

It came from a great God filled with mercy and love.

A very important phase of my illness was about to end. I was afraid. I had grown to accept my changing world in this distant place. I knew how to function in this limited space. I suddenly felt alone. Maybe the real support and love I had been feeling was just a temporary, passing pity.

I was just beginning to climb my mountain, and I knew I could never do it alone. I was now totally dependent as a person. How was I going to function in the faster-moving world back in Dodge City? It seemed so strange to me now; it wasn't the same place that I had once known. An inner strength seemed suddenly to reach out and hold me tightly. I was going to leave the hospital, whether the world and I were ready for a "different model" of Sue or not.

My exit was a celebration, with balloons flying from my wheelchair. My nieces and nephews, with their parents, lined the sidewalk. Before I was loaded into the waiting car, my four-year-old niece Cari handed me a very special pink carnation with a note saying, "We love you, Sue." She then planted one wet good-bye kiss on my cheek. I watched them through the car window as they wildly waved until we were out of sight.

I knew then, without a doubt, I was not alone.

Our small caravan, consisting of four people (Gary, Shawn, my mom, and myself) and two cars, all headed back to Dodge City. The trip home seemed infinite, the miles stretching on and on. Though I was taking this trip sitting up, looking out the windows at the country flying by was impossible for my head to adjust to. With nothing to do but stare at the floor, I quizzed a laughing Gary continually, seeking to know how much further until we would reach our destination.

He was sincerely grateful to be bringing me home, though inwardly he was fighting thoughts of discouragement. He had been so certain that I was going to be able to walk from the hospital, but I still couldn't. He now had a constant fear: Maybe Sue will never walk again. He told himself, "I must believe she will, and keep fighting along with her no matter how long it takes."

Though I had been able to get around with a walker in the therapy sessions, I wasn't able to make my feet cooperate. I hadn't mastered the "walker waltz," though I fondly nicknamed the four-legged steel frame "Phyllis," after my Dodge City walking buddy.

We had decided to stop at Pratt, Kansas, to eat lunch at the local McDonald's. Everyone, including myself, had been so pleased with my progress, we had forgotten some of the problems that still existed. I had forgotten that I might appear somehow strange to those who had never seen me before.

I staggered into McDonald's with the help of Mom and Gary on each arm. It was good to be in the "normal" world again, where most people live. I, too, had once been a part of this world, which now seemed so fast-paced to me.

I was balancing myself between the wall and my mom as we made our way slowly to the restroom. When we entered the restroom, suddenly everyone had moved out of the way, making a path and letting me at the front of the line. I had never thought of myself as ill, and suddenly I was aware that everyone around thought of me that way.

I had been so pleased with my improvement. Although I had a steep mountain ahead of me, I was moving upward. But suddenly I was seeing myself in a different way. I wasn't looking at how far I had come; I was seeing myself through the eyes of those around me.

Later, while we ate, I felt cold chills down my back as I tried to focus on those seated around us in that dining room. They had no idea what I had been through in the last few short weeks.

Sitting there, my mind drifted back to a course I had once taken while working on my master's degree. It had been an in-depth study of unfortunate people who are somehow considered different from those of us who think of ourselves as "normal." We had talked of the many problems one must face when he is labeled as "handicapped." Suddenly I was forced to put a label on myself. No one had said anything in that room, at least that I could hear, nor did they have to. Even with a patch over one eye, I couldn't miss their quick glances, and the curious, innocent stares of the children. Inside I was screaming. I wanted to yell so everyone could hear, "This really isn't me!" I wasn't ready to accept myself as I had become, and somehow I knew the world couldn't.

There had been a time earlier in my life when, like all teens, I had a great deal of difficulty accepting all the parts of my body. I had known God had surely made an error somewhere when He was putting all my parts together. He had made a few of them bigger than I would have issued.

I couldn't hide the anxiety of my situation from my all-knowing Mom. Somehow, since my beginning in this world, I had known of her power and gift to read all five of her children's thoughts like a book. She took the time and energy to deeply know all of her children, even without the assistance of Dr. Spock. She felt all their pain and took it on as if it were her own. I considered her not only "just my mom," but a good friend. My feelings and insecurities couldn't be hidden from her.

She was aware of how self-conscious I felt about eating in front of people. Getting the food to my mouth, without its taking a detour to my nose, was an accomplishment. She quietly reassured me, "No one knows what you have gone through, or they would think you look great, like we do."

My hair had been in long curls before I had become ill. It was difficult for those caring for me to handle me without constantly pulling or getting tangled in the long strands. Since it was a constant "pain" to them as well as for me, I had asked my sister, Debi, to cut it off. This project had been conducted while I had been lying in my Wichita hospital bed. I was deeply saddened as I felt the curls I had labored so long to grow being chopped from my head. Debi had done the best job she could, not being a trained beautician. My unique hospital hair clip, along with the eye patch, mixed with the multiple physical problems I was having, were creating many quick double looks in McDonald's, and I sensed I was making people very uneasy.

All this made me wonder even more if I would be accepted once we arrived in Dodge City.

CHAPTER 10

It all seemed the same to Gary as we arrived at our Dodge City home. Everything emerged clean and shiny after Gary's secretary and church members collected the dust we had compiled in the seventeen long days since our present calamity began.

As Gary looked around the spacious house, it was the same; but he knew those living behind its red brick walls would never be the same again. What was this going to do to us as a family? We must fight the M.S. together, but how? He didn't want to believe Sue might always be this way.

After our arrival, Shawn ran down to the Stephenson's home to let Jason and Phyllis know our car had arrived safely at the parsonage. Phyllis was well-stocked with hugs of excitement as she entered the house, but Jason was quiet and withdrawn as he saw me.

My face was swollen and puffy from the A.C.T.H.

I could see a little out of my one remaining unpatched eye, though everything appeared hazy and blurred. It was very evident to everyone that my depth perception definitely had a "short" in it. For example, consider the ceiling fan in the middle of our living room. Every time people stood up in the center of the room, I was sure they were about to be beheaded by the fast-moving blades. I felt I had saved yet another life as I let out a scream that caused the hearts of all assembled to skip a few beats.

I was very sensitive to the slightest noise. The sound would enter my head and seem to just bounce back and forth. I soon found my nerves and I were not able to tolerate any noise. The clanging of silverware on the table was like the noise of a loud rock band. The everyday noises seemed to enter my ears, but somehow forgot to leave, creating the constant roar of a near-by waterfall, which seemed to be drawing me close to its edge.

My speech was labored and hard to translate into any known speakable English language. This was not all a mouth-related problem. My mind, too, had been badly shaken up; and much of my present memory was gone, as if a giant sponge had soaked up thirty-five years of my accumulated trivia.

I still wasn't able to walk. My hands were useless, except just to keep squeezing the therapeutic balls. All the muscle tone was leaving my limbs, causing them to appear almost dead as they hung lifeless from my body. My ever present companion, fatigue, seemed to be pulling harder and harder at me as though it were trying to suck the last remaining bit of life from my already-defeated body. This produced an extemely heavy feeling which was accompanied by the sensation of a tightly-bound band, or elastic strap, fastened not only around my head and feet, but also my chest and face. It felt like the air I was breathing was being slowly squeezed out of my lungs.

The A.C.T.H. made me feel as a drunk must feel, causing me to view my present, grave situation somewhat more casually than those around me. This, combined

with my extreme gratitude to the Lord and the new view
of life He had given me, could not be dispelled even by the
damaged body into which I was now locked. However, it
was too much to expect Jason to share in the same
gratitude. He couldn't overlook all the problems I was
having for the present. Although he was bodily there, the
rest of him, the part that makes him "Jason," turned and
raced back to where he had been staying, and the security
of another mother, Phyllis. She felt his deep hurt. Knowing I was unable to supply the security he needed, she
allowed her home to become his needed sanctuary. There
he was surrounded by the love and security he needed.

Shannon had been staying with Gary's parents
and didn't get home for several days. She, too, found it
difficult to deal with my inability to be her mother at the
present time. Waves of anger often became her master as
she entered the room where I lay. Looking for a place to
sit, she would throw my legs from the couch, seeming not
to know or care that I had no control of my limbs. She
seemed to want to be near me, yet somehow hurt or get
even with me for the pain my illness was causing her.

Through the years, we had always been extremely
close. We had been much more than mother and
daughter; we had been friends. The thoughts in my head
were clear, at least to me, but there was no way for me to
express them to anyone, not even Shannon. It was as
though I were plugged into a presence who explained to
me each thing that was happening to me and to those
around me, and yet I was powerless to tell anyone, or
comfort them with their load of pain.

I was distantly aware of Shannon's feelings,
though somehow I couldn't reach her. Through this crisis
I had seen her emerge into a different, almost bitter
person. She had always been loving, concerned, and
sympathetic; always one to offer any needed comfort and
encouragement. Though I don't think of myself as pos-
sessing any of these beautiful qualities, perhaps she had
found them deep within me. Perhaps we were creating a

"little Sue," and because of her good nature she had allowed us to repress "Shannon."

Our crisis had dropped a bomb in our home. When any bomb is dropped, there are victims, and this was no exception. People's hearts were bleeding and in extreme pain. I kept telling myself, the Lord would not have allowed this to happen to us if it were going to ruin my family. The Lord promised He would not allow us to be tempted beyond what we could take. Many times this promise was all I had to hang on to, but I had to keep believing it.

Shannon was feeling her own pain over her loss, and it was too much for her to deal with, especially at ten years old. Since I had changed, to get even with me, she too would change. Though wise beyond her years, this situation brought out the "little girl" in her. "Hasn't Mom always been in control before? Somehow she must be responsible for this," she must have reasoned. She and Jason also had a feeling that they personally must be responsible for Mom's illness—maybe if they had behaved better, this wouldn't have happened.

We hadn't left all of our burdens and tensions in the Wichita hospital. Each of us in our own way had to cope with our little crisis. Our trauma was affecting not only us five Wingets, but my parents, sisters and brother; Phyllis; our church family; and friends who had at some time touched our lives.

All had to deal with their own particular grief in different ways. Gary was pulled in many directions trying to be both mother and father, as well as husband and pastor. I wasn't able to do any of the giving in our relationship, being mentally and physically very much like a child. Not only was he caring for three children; now he had a fourth child, me.

My parents were also helping to "re-raise" me, a job they thought they had already completed by the time I reached thirty-five years of age. Their pain was as deep and real as Gary's, as they fought hard and tirelessly to help us climb our mountain.

Each time I went to physical therapy, Phyllis was determined to go with me to be my head cheerleader, something that had been hidden since her high school years. I daily looked forward to her encouraging visits. She was somehow able to put up with my childlikeness and encourage me emotionally and physically. The Lord must have appointed her as my "personal shot-in-the-arm angel."

Our Dodge City church family made arrangements to bring food daily. Though all the visitors greatly lifted my spirits, and erased all my doubt about being accepted, Gary put a limit on my social life (much to my disappointment). Though I hated to admit it, all the excitement from my company only caused my physical problems to become more intense, especially increasing the fatigue.

Norma Jarrett, a registered nurse and member of our church, came in daily for two weeks to give me the A.C.T.H. injections. She was concerned when I couldn't feel the inch-and-a-half needle being inserted. I was more concerned when I saw just how long the needle was. After she gave me the injection the following day in the "even day hip," she knew the feeling must be gone only in my right side, because I felt this needle very keenly.

My role in this drama was to try to fight through the waves of fatigue, pushing myself when there was no energy left even in my reserve tanks. I had to keep digging deep within just to find the energy to be moved from the couch to the chair. It took me days to recover from each session of physical therapy, and then it was time to go once again. When I lay there too exhausted to raise the heaviness of my arms or legs, I had to constantly remind myself that my strength would come from the Lord, not from within: "But they that wait upon the Lord shall renew their strength. They shall mount up with wings like eagles; they shall run and not be weary; they shall walk and not faint" Isaiah 40:31 (TLB). I must give my best to the Lord, so He could give me back His best.

Being dependent upon others wasn't a situation I handled well. Perhaps this was one of the many lessons I was to learn. Once I was placed in bed, I was a prisoner until someone chose to retrieve me, a frequent problem experienced by most infants. Though I had been guilty of saying it would be interesting to have a chance to live my life over again, I never dreamed of doing it quite like this. Like an infant, I would have to learn to sit, talk, walk and experience life once again. One could say one life had ended and a new one begun. I had begun a new life when I became a Christian at the age of seventeen. This too was going to be a new beginning. I must be patient as I lived my life, a miracle in progress.

CHAPTER 11

     Mom stayed with us for several more days until she was called home on business. She had been gone over a month and there were many decisions to be made on the new home the folks were building, and they had put it on hold as long as they could. Since I was continually improving, though it was difficult for her to tear herself away, she left her clothes in the closet and pillow on the bed as a symbolic gesture of her return. She was concerned that she might miss out on some vital part of my recovery. We assured her we would let her know of any super important events (such as my first tooth). Phyllis promised she would keep both her eyes on me, and report any changes.

     The members of the church quickly jumped in with a "Help Sue List" complete with "people sitters" to relieve Gary so he could go to the office two hours in the mornings and afternoons.

Since we had been in the church such a short time, I didn't know very many people, and they didn't know me. They felt this was a good time to get to know me. It's very difficult to ask someone you just met to take you to the bathroom. Because of the A.C.T.H., my kidneys were not working properly, and having fluids build up in my body was a problem. I needed to be moved or walked at least every hour. I was needing more care than any of these beautiful people were trained to give me. The children wanted to care for me alone, hoping to get our family back to normal. They couldn't fully understand the reality that they weren't ready to be totally responsible for my life.

One Wednesday night they were left to "mother sit" one hour while Gary went to church. After Gary left, they too retreated, leaving me unattended. Because of my sensitivity to noise, the children found it very difficult to be around me. I was extremely emotional. I was either laughing or yelling. I was slowly driving them away from me; so usually, rather than be around me and be yelled at, they found something to do somewhere else. When dad arrived on the scene, he found me in tears. No children were around and I had crawled to the bathroom. Crawling can be difficult when you are in *good* shape! Gary was very angry with the situation he found. A family meeting was immediately called, and the children were summoned from every corner of their worlds.

Our meeting was to be held on the front porch. I was feeling very much like a burden to my family. Because of the extensive care that I was needing, I told Gary, "I think it might be of benefit to all of you if I were put in a rehabilitation home somewhere."

Gary was deeply hurt by my suggestion. He thought I didn't feel his efforts of caring for me were good enough. Totally frustrated by the pressures of my illness, home, and the church, he began to cry. Thinking my needs were not being met, he sobbed, "I'm trying to do my best for you, Sue." The children sat motionless, feeling guilty because they hadn't followed through on their "mother sitting" responsibilities and angry with their siblings for not doing it.

Our little family meeting turned into a "family cry," sitting on our front porch, probably making the whole neighborhood uncomfortable. There was a growing pain in my chest, not caused by the M.S. It was an ache in my heart that no pain medication could possibly reach. I was deeply hurting because my children were already beginning to label me as the source of all our present problems. It was difficult for my family and for me to blame the true villain of my illness, the M.S. Not only were they victims of this unfair situation, but so was I.

Our family meeting was still in session, but no words were being spoken. Tears still flowing down the members' cheeks, Phyllis walked up on the porch and took my hand. After she had calmed us all, she suggested that she and I try to take our walk. As we left, the "meeting" was discontinued....

I'm not sure Phyllis and my "walk" fit the typical definition of a walk. After I had been home from the hospital a few days, Phyllis encouraged me to see how far I could walk. She knew how important walking had been to me in my "other life." Leaning heavily against her, with my arms extended in front of me for any possible balance, she held me tightly—so tightly it left marks on my arm. Together we stumbled, each step an effort for both of us. The first night we didn't make it any farther than the end of the driveway, a far distance from the four miles I was used to walking a day. Each night we would try to make it a few steps further. Many times Phyllis was almost carrying me by the time we got back home.

The whole neighborhood was secretly cheering us on as they watched us reach every mini-goal, but it was a giant accomplishment to Phyllis and my family. I would have to push aside my exhaustion, unsure if I could find the energy to fight through another battle just to walk those few short feet. Phyllis literally used all her energy to drag me home and pour me into the chair.

My life consisted of basically rest, therapy, and more rest. My therapy was three exhausting sessions a week; the rest of the time I just rested to be ready for therapy again. We were excited over the progress I was making in the sessions.

The Lord had put yet another special person in my life, my physical therapist, Melaney McWhirt. She made what could have been a boring experience fun. She worked me hard, but combined the sit-ups and other exercises with time-out for laughter.

"Sue came to Humana Hospital - Dodge City for physical therapy on July 9, 1984," Melaney remembered. Continuing, she stated, "An initial evaluation was done to determine her capabilities. Sue reported to me that she initially had blurred vision and numbness on her right side. After being transferred to Wesley she was 'like jelly.' Physical therapy was begun in Wesley and she progressed to the point where she could ambulate with help. Her primary complaints on her initial visit to me were a ringing in her ears and double vision. The double vision required wearing a patch over one eye, alternating each day. In her physical activities, Sue's balance proved difficult. If she started to fall, there was no way to catch herself.

"My evaluation of Sue's capabilities found her to have a generalized decrease in strength and endurance. The right side of her body was slightly weaker than the left. Coordination was fair in fine motor movements. Balance and protective reactions were delayed. Her gait was what we call ataxic, meaning lacking muscle coordination. She walked unsteadily; her foot placement was inconsistent; and she would weave from side to side. From the evaluation, I found that there were numerous things to work on.

"One of our main goals for Sue was for her to ambulate independently with or without an assistive device. At Wesley Hospital she began walking with a walker, but preferred walking with someone. An attempt at using a wide-based cane was unsuccessful early on. Sue wanted to walk totally unassisted, so activities were designed to reach that goal.

"It was a pleasure to work with Sue. It's refreshing to have someone whose faith, positive attitude, and willingness to work help achieve the goal you both want to reach."

I continued to wear an eye patch, seeing double for over a month. Just before Phyllis was to pick me up for my workout in therapy, I asked Gary to call for prayer. Since I couldn't go to the phone to share in their prayer, Gary and Jason formed a "clothesline" holding hands across the room until they could reach mine. Together the three of us prayed with the counselor on the phone, believing in my miracle. When I first became ill, I had wondered if I had to choose just one of the symptoms to be corrected, which would it be? It was a question I could not resolve. It was now the eighteenth of July, and I had been seeing two of everything since June 17th. After we prayed, I felt a strong inner urging to take off the patch. I had still needed it that morning when I awoke. Now when I removed it, the double vision was gone. Now all of us knew we must be patient—there was a miracle in progress.

Every victory seems to be closely followed by discouragement. When Norma came to give me my shot the next day, she found my feet were swelling from the fluid my body was retaining. The cramping in my legs and feet was more frequent and severe. As my feet cramped it felt like the bones were being crushed in a vise. Rubbing and massaging had always lessened the cramping, but now it only made the pain more intense. The x-ray showed no break, but I was told to begin moving around more to get my kidneys functioning properly.

Mom came back after being gone a week, and she could already see improvement. I had steadily made advancements. I had finished my fourteen shots of A.C.T.H. I had feeling in both my "even and odd day hips." Certainly, it was a small thing to be thankful for, but it was progress nevertheless. Though my vision was still badly affected, I now saw only one of everything. I was working hard in therapy sessions, and my right side seemed to be getting stronger each day. My left side, though affected, was much stronger than my right.

Some friends, the Hetricks, had flown my parents from Topeka to Dodge City in their small plane. They were all pleased to see me doing so well, and surprised to see me progressing so quickly. It appeared as though I were improving weeks or months each day, which might account for the fact that each day seemed weeks long.

Gary, Phyllis, Mom and Dad, and I were all caught up in our joy over my improvement. We had been told there might be some bad days, which we had expected, but none of us had prepared ourselves for the possibility I would do anything but improve. Four days after the series of shots had been discontinued, I felt as though I were slipping away from reality again, as I had done when I first became ill. When I tried to share this feeling with Mom and Gary, they wouldn't accept it as out of the ordinary for me.

Denial and fear can often keep one from seeing and accepting the truth. I *was* slipping slowly away again. My head was aching and it was becoming more difficult for me to speak. Mom and Gary were trying not to overreact to the situation. Being with me every moment, it was difficult to notice any gradual change.

The following day it was easy to convince my therapist, Melaney, there was something wrong. It was easier for her to see the change just in my talking alone, when she wasn't with me every day. My head was hurting and my speech had deteriorated to the way it had been in Wichita. It took two people to handle me when I walked now. Melaney found I had lost all the strength I had gained in my right side. Since the new attack, I had lost control of my left side also; it was weaker than my right side now. We would have to begin all over. It also weakened the muscles in my bladder, leaving me with no bladder control. Melaney suggested we get in touch with the doctor right away. Dr. Johnson was in the hospital, and he put me on eighty units of Prednisone, a medication often used for M.S.

CHAPTER 12

It was easy to believe in a miracle when everything was moving forward. It was definitely more difficult to keep believing when things looked so black. Even our doctor from Wichita called and told Gary he was very sorry, but maybe this was as far as I would progress.

I was aware faith is not what we can see or even think exists. Faith cannot afford to be negative, although it has its down days. Like Peter when he walked on the water, I too, could sink—especially when I looked down at my impossible situation. Like Peter, I needed to look up into the face of my Savior, Jesus. I had to keep my eyes fixed upon Him and walk on top of my impossible situation. With my eyes constantly fixed on Him, I could not give up when the water was really rough. That was when faith had a chance to spring forth. My faith was being challenged to the limits. I had been given an opportunity to prove that my faith in the Lord was not only real, but powerful.

Scripture says about faith: "What is faith? It is the confident assurance that something is going to happen. It is the certainty that what we hope for is waiting for us, even though we cannot see ahead" Hebrews 11:1 (TLB).

It took me awhile to get my faith "all together." I was afraid, afraid of what the morning light would bring. It had been very peaceful when I approached death's door before. Now I was terrified at the thought of finding myself there once again; yet I was more afraid of finding myself in the same physical condition as when I first went to Wichita.

When I shared my fear with Gary, he bought me a giant-print Bible. As he handed me the book, it was so big and bulky I almost dropped it. I began leafing through the pages, but it was too difficult for me to read the words, until I found the Psalms. The words didn't seem so close together because the format was different. I was immediately comforted by the writing of a man who had found himself surrounded by trials and troubles, as he cried loudly unto the Lord.

"O Lord, so many are against me. So many seek to harm me. [The M.S. was trying to destroy me.] I have so many enemies. So many say that God will never help me. [How true!] But Lord, you are my shield, my glory, and my only hope. [Even my doctors have given up hope.] You alone can lift my head, now bowed in shame.

"I cry out to the Lord and he heard me from his Temple in Jerusalem. Then I lay down and slept in peace and woke up safely, for the Lord was watching over me. And now, although ten thousand enemies surround me on every side, I am not afraid" Psalm 3:1-6 (TLB).

Peace flowed through my body, and my fear melted away like snow. I was at peace, and for the first time I knew my God was big enough to fight any problem I could present to Him. I had a big God and I was confident He and I could conquer any problem thrown in our path. As the

98

Psalmist said, I was no longer afraid. For the first time in days, I slept in peace, unafraid of what tomorrow would bring.

The definite change in my attitude was plain for those around me to see. Even those who hadn't seen me for several days questioned what had made the change. I had been a Christian for over twenty years, and usually was on good speaking terms, I had thought, with the Lord; but walking in total faith was a new journey for me.

"All who are oppressed may come to him. He is a refuge for them in their times of trouble. All those who know your mercy, Lord, will count on you for help. For you have never yet forsaken those who trust in you" Psalm 9:9, 10 (TLB).

Though several different medical recipes had been prescribed to be injected or swallowed, walking in faith was pulling me above the M.S., making each step of my heavy legs lighter.

Still another good recipe was Phyllis' survival formula. It, too, was one that kept me going many days when I felt engulfed by my tangled world. It had been practiced by Bob and Phyllis as they tried to weather the storm of his struggle against cancer.

First, it was understood that those caring or visiting do not want to be around a continually depressed, discouraged, pessimistic patient. This was understandable even to me in my somewhat scrambled state of mind; nor did I, as the patient, want to be around any such negative beasts either. Not only must I attempt to have a positive attitude, but it was vitally important to my recovery that I be surrounded with positive people. Those caring for me often sheltered me from the discouraging verbal blows issued by these often well-meaning contrary folk.

Second, I and those directly involved with me were allowed two (just two) "down days" a week. I found this permission to be "down" valuable to me. Rarely did I need both days. One day usually was sufficient to help me release all the tears I had bottled up, and do all the pouting I had the energy for.

Laughter, too, was playing a gigantic part in my recovery. We were told the A.C.T.H., which we had fondly labeled as my "laughing juice," might make me a little moody. We soon found the Prednisone had the same effects. Though I could be pulled down easily by the children's changeable moods and opinions, I was constantly aware that my attitude was very important to my recovery, just as our doctor in Wichita had said. I, too, strongly believed it. I also believed that one's attitude is often plugged into a source which can power us. My source of power was also my best friend, Jesus Christ.

Laughing was one of the pleasant side effects which can be caused by the drug. Even though my face was puffy and swollen, I was spared any of the serious complications that often are expected from this strong drug. I was told it would take me a week before the drug could be absorbed into my body, but I was responding within two or three days. Could the Lord be using the medication, along with the touch of His hand, I wondered? We had sought His guidance when we had shopped for doctors. Since we believe these doctors were His pick of the litter, we must trust Him now to be the Head Physician and lead and advise the team.

I didn't mind all the hard work in physical therapy. It drained me of any energy, but I always seemed to be able to do the exercise one more time, with the hope that it would bring me one step closer to my miracle. I knew I was not earning my miracle. The simple fact that I mustered the strength to even do one exercise was proof enough to me that somebody else had His hand on me.

Writing was a different story entirely. I had to push and make myself use my hands. My handwriting was messy and very difficult to read. It would have ranked right up there with the kindergarteners who couldn't master pencil pushing. It was difficult to go back to the frustrating days when the pencil seemed to have a mind all of its own. Like an untamed rodeo horse, it would jump around wildly in my hand. It would take days, weeks, months, maybe even years to get the wild animal to yield to my control. No way! I wasn't about to go through that frustrating experience. As in my kindergarten years, my mom had different thoughts on the subject. She was determined I would at least learn to write my name once again, so I would be able to sign a check, a task she felt every "red-blooded American housewife" should be able to perform.

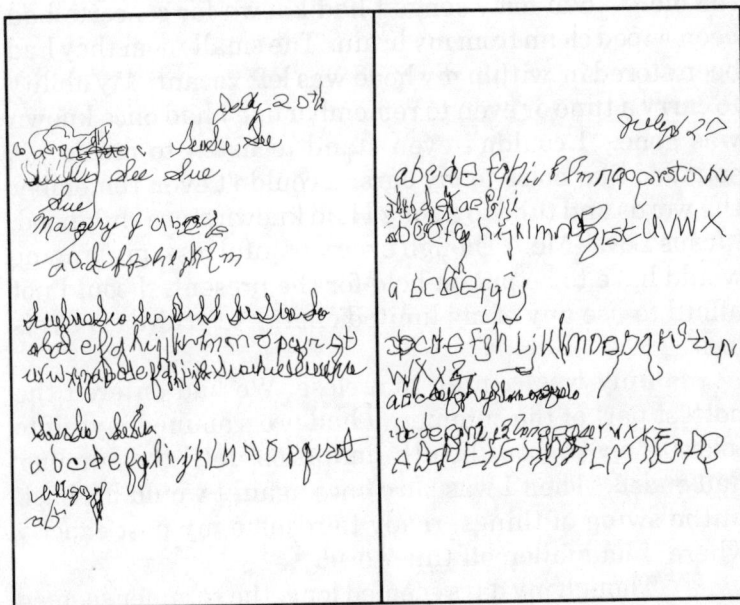

a bcdefghijhlmhopqrstu v w xyz   Aug 1
Sue Winget Sue Winget Sue Winget
Merry Christmas August August
August August Happy Birthday baby Doll
a bcde fg hi jklmnopqo qooooooo ooooo
Marge Hogue ~ Marge Hogue
Aug 2
a bcdef g hi jklm nopqrstuvwxy q
Sue Winget Sue Winget Sue Winget
Jason Winget Jason Winget
qqqqo ooo qqqqqqqoqq qqqq

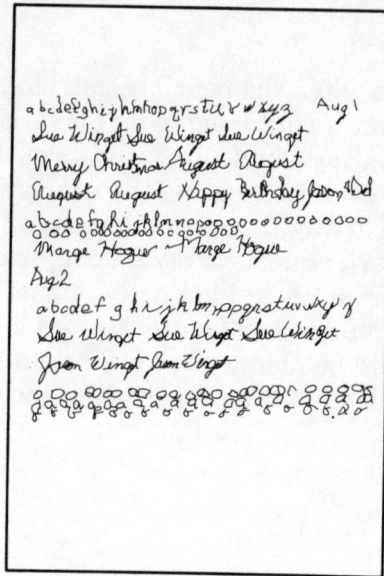

Another source of distraction and intense grief was
from my singing: it was completely gone. All the words to
the more than forty songs I had known for concerts had
been wiped clean from my brain. The small room they had
been stored in within my head was left vacant. My ability
to carry a tune or even to remember one I had once known
was gone. I couldn't even stand to listen to music. It
sounded like noise to my ears. I couldn't even remember
the words and tune to a song I had known since childhood,
"Jesus Loves Me." Though a very painful loss, my singing
would have to be put on hold for the present. I could not
afford to use any of my limited energy to grieve over this
loss.

July was coming to a close. We had entered the
hottest part of the summer. I had programmed myself to
tolerate my present health limitation until the summer
had ended. Then I was sure once again I would be back
in the swing of things, ready to resume my post exactly
where I had fallen off this world.

Though my days seemed long, the summer seemed
to be flowing from week to week, as if there were a master
plan or Master Planner in charge of my social calendar.

New adventures, and usually some distant visitors, found their way to our door. Though many times Gary was afraid their visit would tire me too much, each one seemed to lift me from the depths of my physical problems. Each seemed to bring a special gift, an added strength and encouragement, all building the number of members of our fast-growing army climbing our mountain toward our miracle. This encouraged me to be constantly looking up, hopeful we might soon reach the top.

I looked forward daily to the arrival of our mail. I had already received over two hundred cards and letters. I was overwhelmed by the support of old and new friends showering me with their loving support. Each card was placed in a basket in the living room and our basket was literally overflowing with support. I couldn't look at the "love basket" without feeling the tremendous support and love as it carried me through each day. Possibly just a simple card to the one who had sent it, it was a little piece of hope to me.

Another thing I looked forward to each day was the arrival of Phyllis. She came to get me almost daily for our walks. She seemed to have taken my recovery so personally! I was learning from her a new and deeper definition of the term "friend." I couldn't help but be lifted by her, as she climbed my mountain by my side. The Lord had placed this woman in my path at just the right time and place.

My dependence was growing, causing this strong lady only to feel a deeper burden and stronger sense of responsibility toward me. Our lives were becoming more tightly intertwined as she tried to relieve Gary from some of the burden of my care. Although my illness was causing an exciting and eventful summer in place of the numbing one she had feared, it was still difficult. I was unable to think much beyond myself, and so this left Phyllis alone to handle her own grief.

It was difficult to deal with me on the emotional and mental level of my present state of being. Would I

103

have had the inner strength to be the friend she was being? Maybe she would be pushed to the breaking point. I couldn't help fearing for our short friendship. She was having to do all the giving, something I had been used to doing in my relationships.

"[Jesus]...took the blind man by the hand and led him...."

-Mark 8:23

CHAPTER 13

Writing and using my hands was my greatest frustration. I had attempted to scribble the A,B,C,'s until I detested each letter.

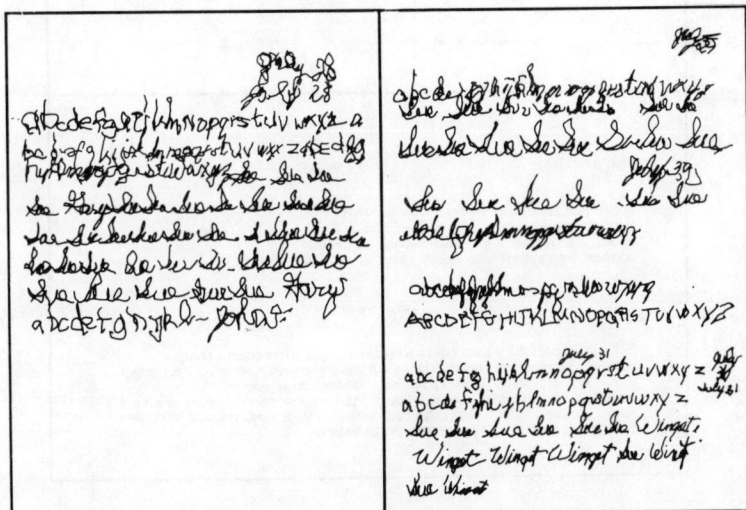

I had been working with an antique manual type-writer that I have no doubt didn't know how to type. In my "other life," typing was never a talent I had been issued. Why I was required in my present state to wrestle with a machine I hadn't been able to master since birth, I will perhaps never be sure. Typing over and over the musical familiar saying, "Now is the time for all good men to come to the aid of their party." This, along with my constant repetition of 'our beloved' A,B,C,'s was creating a constructive release valve for my bottled-up anger, as I pounded away. I'm certain little wisps of smoke could be seen ascending not only from my ears, but also from the keys of that vengeful creature, with a stronger will than even I possessed.

```
     n w isthe time fo r all goind men to  ome to the aid ift hee aid of

     theirr pparty.   Now is the time for  all     hood men to come to the
     aid of their party.

     You can tellty

     Dear Phylli is,

     Thistypewritier and I are nnotfriends do not kno w if I ever
     ytyped on amanual  e  re  Donot tthink   I amnow.

     Thi s i s t he p t s

     guess I ca n t blame t his forever

          August 2

               Lo ve S ue
```

```
     Dear phyllis,              fri., August 3rd.

     Today has been a good day.  But I don't t hink my typing is any
     better.  Maybe after a feww weeks of f t this I sho uld improve, who
     knows.  H owever I do nndat yuhdnk we should ever judge my improve-
     ment by my typing!  It would jjust be too  depressing.

               Love - Sue

          abcdefghijklmno pqrstuvwxyzabcdefghijklmnopqarstuvwxyza
     bcdefghijklmnopqrdtuvwxyzabcdefghijklmnopqrstuvwxyzabcdefghijklmnopqrs
     t uvw xyz abcdefghijklmnozqratuvwxy  abcdefghijklmbo pq rstuvwxyz
     abcdef ghijklmnopqrsttuvwsyz  Now is the tt ime for all good men to
     come  to the aid oof their party.  NOW S  TH E TIME FOR ALL GOOD MEN
     TO COME TO THE AID OFF TXHEREX THEIR PARTY .
```

To try to diminish my agony , Phyllis suggested I type her a daily letter. It took extreme talent and imagination to interpret these works of art! Spelling had been forgotten, as well as other data, from trivia to information facts, such as how long Gary and I had been married. Between my poor spelling and definite lack of typing skill, my letters were extremely laughable—but they came from the depths of my hurting soul.

```
                    August 4th  -Saturday
        Dezr Phykkis,

        Nomo re cracks abo ut my typing, because we both k
        know it  is bad.  Guess I don' t have t o wvorry b
        about anyo ne wanting us for their secretary
        This type is so light I can not read it.
        Maybe, just maybe the Lord wan s me t o learn to'
        type. why, I doo not kno w,1/21/2(G ary tried to'
        fix this typewriter,but I think it has a mind of its o
        own. the bell is not working, I just can not
        imagine any one wanting to be a secretary.  It
        would take a special person.

                        Love,  Sue
```

```
    Au gust22,

    Dear Phyllis,

            The therapist hhouught I Should usse the manuA  I
    typewritter.  Znd needlessa to say we gfight alot.
    I don't even think it spells in English.
            Tonight is Wednesday night church, and I hope
    I will beegoing before long.  Gary wants me tpgo
    to the film Sunday nighr,but I don't know if I am up to that.  maybe,
    by then the  noise will not bother me.
            Today the dr. cut a mole off  my back,not be-
    cause it was bothering me, but because it bothered my mom a and
    sister.
            Hope you are enjoying your trip.  We really en-
    joyed our wellsville company.  She went with mme to
    therapy.  The therapist was really almiracle,that I ask
    her she said it was really just    a mira cle that
    I had inproved so much.
            Guess thre lord just is not going to give us any miracles on my
    typing.

                    love sue,
```

```
    Dear Phyllis,
            I am really excited today.  I don't knos if I can explain it all
    to you. Espedially uf  I have to ty pe it.  Last nite was rhe first
    time I  really went to sleep with o ut being afraid.  For t he first
    time I REALLY felt like th3 thhe Lord was with me.  He really is
    bigger t han any enemy I have to- face.
    I guess I REALLY did not believe t hat.  I read that bible and
    psalms:3:5-8 (especially 5) ministered to me,  It was just what I
    needed.  I can n't tell yoou t he feeling of overwhelming love I felt
    f or the first time. oops --Ho pe I am no t preaching- just want to
    share what I am experiencing with you.

            LOVE -- SUE
```

Many times my letter took the form of a prayer which was shared just between me and the Lord....

Thus ends the reading of the scroll of the "Epistles of Sue."

CHAPTER 14

"I will fear no evil: for thou art with me" (Psalm 23:4b).

Wall-walking was becoming my everyday practice, as I inched along the wall seeking to reach my destination. Like all toddlers, I wasn't able to make my journey any further than a few steps from an immovable object without losing my balance.   Each step was unsure and insecure. I was having to learn that I would have to take it one step at a time. The time had come when I could take on any one-year old! I have to admit I had an unfair advantage: I had been through this once before.

I could identify with both infants and elderly as I battled the fear of falling. Each time the subject of the walker or canes for more stability was brought up, something inside of me seemed to stand up and begin cheering. Loud and strong, the voice chanted like a crowd at a football game. "No-oo-oo - I - will - walk! No - I - will - walk! No - I - will - walk!"

My stubborn Scotch Irish blood, combined with my half-hearted attempts and lack of balance, made all my practice futile. Maybe if there had been a six- or eight-legged walker instead of the standard four-footed critter, I could, or would have, mastered it. I was shocked when I found out that a four-footed cane was made now!

Phyllis was not only helping me re-learn to walk, but she was often my right as well as my left hand. She only handled one position when my mom was in town, but she was quick to pick up the dropped hand when Mom left. My parents both were making frequent trips to and from Dodge City. Not more than two weeks could pass by without them checking in to make sure my progress was still forward.

When I needed her, Phyllis was always on deck. She washed my hair and filed my nails, when they became a lethal length. She even plucked my eyebrows before they grew together as one large "brow." These tasks, though little, were important for what little self-image I could muster, and most of all, important to me even though I couldn't see her finished work. The very last thing I would do was to turn Gary loose with the tweezers. His first and last attempt at my grooming had been in Wesley Hospital when he ventured to brush my teeth. I am aware it's difficult to brush someone else's teeth. Gary had never had braces in his life, although he did have teeth. His struggle to remove the evening's lasagna from my tin-covered teeth was an experience neither one of us will forget. I have decided from this experience that I will not trust him with my teeth again until the day comes in our future that I can take them out and hand them to him!

One thing I did have to learn when cleaning my teeth: Don't turn the Water-pik on until the end that sprays the water is safely anchored in your mouth! (The bathroom will never be the same....)

Re-learning can be a lot of fun, if your sense of

110

humor doesn't weaken!

"He will yet fill your mouth with laughter and your
lips with shouts of joy" (Job 8:21).

Laughter was one way of releasing the inner pain:

O Lord, do not rebuke me in your anger or disci-
pline me in your wrath.
Be merciful to me, Lord, for I am faint;
O heal me for my bones are in anguish.
How long, O Lord, how long?
Turn, O Lord, and deliver me;
Save me because of your unfailing love.
No one remembers you when he is dead.
Who praises you from the grave?
I am worn out from groaning;
all night long I flood my bed with weeping
and drench my couch with tears.
My eyes grow weak with sorrow;
they fail because of all my foes.
Away from me, all you who do evil,
for the Lord has heard my weeping.
The Lord has heard my cry for mercy;
The Lord accepts my prayer.

Psalm 6 (NIV)

For Gary, trying to balance my illness, working at
the church, and being mother and father to our children,
on top of working on his Doctor of Ministry Degree, was
becoming more than even Gary could handle.

I was needing to go to Central and Eastern Kansas
for doctor and orthodontist appointments and I could be
sent off to my parents in Topeka. The children could be
farmed out somewhere within the state, from Dodge City
to Wellsville. This would give Gary a necessary break.
Though he would never have admitted it, Gary was badly
in need of relief from all the home pressures. So were the

children. My nerves had been badly shaken by the M.S., and it wasn't easy to live with my demands and short fuse. As the children so often said, I was different, a changed person, not the same "good ole mom" who had bossed them around before. They weren't sure they liked the new me. Enough was enough! I was carrying this sick thing just a little too far. They were growing weary of it. I was aware of just how difficult I was to live with. The thing they didn't seem to realize was that I was locked in, trapped with this body. I couldn't just walk away from it anytime I became disgusted with it. How I longed to be released for just a moment of freedom!

My younger sister Debi had come to spend the week with us prior to Gary's going to Chicago. She was a tough cookie! She demanded that I try to act as normal as I could. I was beginning to develop many not so "normal" habits. Walking with one's arms extended straight out for balance, especially when one walks a little strangely anyway, immediately lets others know you are somehow different.

Debi was raising a deaf son. Though she was small and dainty in stature, her life experiences had not only made her compassionate, but had conditioned her for a position as a sergeant in the Marine Corps. "Put down those arms! Stick out your chest! Raise that head!"

My family had been sure I wouldn't be able to care for myself in the fall. Even though I had been making progress, I had so far to come. With the aid of the walls, I was getting around fairly well. Gary and my parents were making plans to hire a "caretaker" for me after the children went back to school in the fall. They still didn't feel I was ready to stay at home by myself. The situation had to be re-evaluated after I completed a week of "boot camp" with sister Debi. Debi's crash course was helping me learn to take care of myself, and to depend more on myself instead of others. It was designed to take the invalid out of the patient. She made me try everything I did at least once before she helped me. She let me make mistakes, even encouraged me to, so at least I was trying. She was very patient, yet one tough lady.

My mom was very excited about my improvement in the short week with Debi. It had taught us all a valuable lesson. It was time for the support from my whole family, not to end, but to take a different trail up my mountain.

It would be different from the trail Gary and I were to climb, but still leading toward the same mountain top. The Lord was slowly preparing to wean me off constant care. Would I be ready? Another phase in His great plan for my miracle was beginning to unfold.

> "There is a time for everything,
>   and a season for every activity under heaven:
>   a time to be born and a time to die,
>   a time to plant and a time to uproot,
>   a time to kill and a time to heal,
>   a time to tear down and a time to build,
>   a time to weep and a time to laugh..."

Ecclesiastes 3:1-4 (NIV)

Debi took me to Wichita for an appointment with Dr. Barnett. Gary stayed reluctantly in Dodge City. Barnett was surprised to see me teeter into his office on my own. Pleased by my progress, he still wanted me to stay on the Prednisone Dr. Johnson had prescribed, until around Christmas.

August 14th was to be a big day for me. Mom was to take me to Kansas City to get my braces off, a big day for any "metal mouth." Although Mom and Gary had felt the experience might be too much for me to tolerate, I was anxiously waiting for the day to finally arrive. Although my braces were to come off, I was to be fitted for retainers.

All that was accomplished was that I traded one problem for another. Those of us who have gotten to wear "tin grins" know the sacrifices of getting food jammed between your teeth at every meal, and not being allowed to chew gum or eat raw fruit or vegetables. Oh, the longing for a raw carrot; a craving I would certainly never have dreamed I would have; pickles—maybe, but carrots—never. Now with a retainer I could eat anything! The only problem was I couldn't get the thing out of my mouth, a task that can only be performed by me, without pulling my teeth out. Then there were days when the thing was so loose that it smacked loudly everytime I moved my tongue, and my speaking voice was seasoned with ss...sss..ss..s's. Though this seemed a little awkward to me, I knew the end result would be payment enough: a smile that would stop approaching traffic.

While in Topeka my mom was determined to keep me typing. It was hard to "dig up" an old manual typewriter since the invention of electricity, but Mom and Dad managed. They were able to find this relic deep within the catacombs of a typewriter shop. When I started banging the keys, nothing happened. Dad turned it upside down and a mouse's nest came tumbling out. The keys had been rusted tightly within their case, caused by years of unuse and maybe our mouse friend. No longer could I even bang out an S.O.S. I would be spared this "therapy," for the rest of my stay at least.

Everyone I have ever known has an Uncle Ed hidden somewhere in their family tree. Mine lives on a farm near Iola, Kansas. Every summer for the last few years we have gone down for a family gathering. This is the time when Uncle Ed makes his rhubarb pie and relatives come from all over the country. This year I tried to tell Mom I wasn't even up to rhubarb pie, let alone a family reunion. I felt I might somehow block the flow of the usual social affair, such as the annual march to the T.G.&Y. department store. She won and I soon found myself on the way to Iola. A couple of memories stand out from that visit.

My old college roommate, Carol Bingle, lives near Iola. Carol had been writing me faithfully since my

114

illness. She was relieved over my progress as she visited with me. It was one of the highlights of my visit when she walked through the door of my motel room. Though I hate to admit it, even to myself, it has been over fifteen years since we roomed together at Sterling College. I didn't get to see her much because we were always separated by distance, but when we were together, the years since our last visit just fell away, and it seemed we had never been apart. True friendship is really a precious gift.

My cousin Sammy speaks with a very strong southern drawl. She felt like I, too, was carrying a strong, almost English accent. She thought it was cute. I assured her it was accompanied by my new English walk, a most distinguished step, or at least it might be if I ever got it mastered.

I had to admit, the family reunion brought many waves of laughter as well as tears of joy, as we shared the same ole family tales of our childhood experiences that we shared each year. In all, it was a great time, but I was anxious to get back to Dodge City.

However, Shannon and Jason were finding it very difficult to appreciate all the different "bosses," as they put it, who entered their lives: my mom, as well as my three sisters who picked up the mother-role that I couldn't fulfill. Shannon and Jason did not appreciate their attempt. They resented them. I knew a time would come in the not-so-distant future that the children would look back and see that these "villains" were heaven-sent. Never would we have made it through those difficult months without all these "bosses." Now it was easy for my young children to turn their anger toward these innocent helpers, blaming them for their lives being blown into little pieces, instead of seeing the true villain as the M.S.

Summer was coming to an end, and it was trying to leave its mark by making one more jab at us with its smoldering rays of sun. School was beginning; and though the kids and most mothers were ready, I wasn't sure I was. Wouldn't everyone soon forget my battle? Had they grown weary from the long, tiresome journey up my mountain? My improvement had been rapid the last two weeks; maybe the Lord knew it was time for Gary and me to climb alone; but I wasn't ready.

On August 24th, I went down to Phyllis' house. We had both been gone for the past two weeks, so we had lots to share. Not knowing my feeling of abandonment, she shared her latest news with me: She had just that day been offered a job with the school system. Deep in my heart I knew she was at a point in her life where she needed to find a new purpose for living. My deep dependence on her was unfair. Maybe I had latched too tightly onto her, seeing her as the strong me I used to be. My dependence on her was like holding on to a part of my old self. I tried to control my feelings as she told me her news, but it was no use. My self-pity took control. My tears were flooding her living room. If she had any joy concerning that job, it was soon drenched along with her carpet. I was being choked by my feelings of loneliness and self-pity. Was this what the Lord had been trying to prepare me for? Somehow, through the sobs, I was trying to reassure Phyllis, and myself, that the Lord must have a purpose in all this. He hadn't brought me through the summer to leave me now. I left and continued my tears for more than the two regular allowed down days. I questioned, Was my illness too much of a load to be piled on this young friendship? Was I to lose this dear friend? Was our friendship to be lost in a world already too busy for relationships? I continued feeling sorry for myself, grieving over what I feared might possibly be the slow death of a friendship lost within the fast-moving pace of this merry-go-round of life.

Birthdays had always been a celebrated event in the life of our family. My birthday fell on the twenty-seventh of August, a day I felt was very important this year. A few short months earlier I had feared I had already lived to see my last year roll around. This birthday, I had a chance to have a new beginning. I was determined nothing would rob me of this special day. The knowledge that I would be aging when this day arrived, a thought that usually caused at least a moment's pause for meditation and adjustment, did not enter my thoughts this year.

My day was filled with a steady flow of cards and gifts. The mailman was weighted down with over sixty as the church surprised me with a card shower for my birthday. Gary was determined to make this a very special day for me, ending with a surprise party with a few close friends. My body was exhausted from the excitement of the day. Just from opening all those cards! Each one was like a step lifting me higher, giving me more courage with each card. This day the love and support of my new friends in our Dodge City church wasn't just sprinkled on me; it was poured, gushing all over and around me.

CHAPTER 15

The long eventful summer was finally over; my three children had found their way back to greet their school chums and lock horns with the educators.

The summer had not made its long journey through the hot months without leaving its victims. I looked at my battle-scarred family, knowing our experience of the past few months would somehow leave its mark on each one of us, but how? I clung tightly to the promise: "And we know that all that happens to us is working for our good if we love God and are fitting into his plans" Romans 8:28 (TLB). Many times others had quoted this verse to me when I wasn't willing to listen, but now it was all I had to hang on to.

The children were soon very involved in school. My nerves had been affected by the illness, and the children found it much more pleasant to keep busy and stay away from home as much as possible. In anger, they often said,

"You aren't the same Mom you were several months ago!"

"You bet I'm not!" I responded. "No one knows that better than I!" I was fighting very hard to restore my self-concept which had been destroyed by my illness. It was difficult to establish any value as a person, when most of the summer I couldn't even go to the bathroom alone! Although I was able to take care of myself more each day, it had been a humbling experience to be so dependent on others to meet my needs.

It had also been difficult to learn to wait for others to fill those needs. Patience was one virtue I lost when I became ill. I found myself very demanding, perhaps because I had nothing to do but sit around and dwell on these needs. My demanding spirit was one reason the children chose to keep some distance between themselves and me.

My days without the children were quiet; not so hard on my ears, but lonely. I looked forward each day to their arrival home from school, longing to hear how the day had gone. To see me was only a reminder of what they had escaped from, earlier in the day, before school. As soon as they made their entrance into the house, they quickly made an exit to avoid my impatient nagging.

With the beginning of school, people drifted back into the groove of their busy schedules. This brought an end to the steady flow of cards and letters that had carried me through the long summer, although their strong support was not forgotten. I knew they would continue the climb with me through their prayer support. Throughout the summer months, there had been over three hundred cards overflowing my "love basket," each brimming with love and encouragement that would carry me through the months ahead.

Often when I received a card, I would recall a favorite childhood record and book, *The Little Engine That Could.* As a child, I had listened again and again to that badly scratched recording. The wise words from the little engine were etched in my mind as he made an attempt to climb his seemingly impossible mountain. He chanted, "I think I can. I think I can. I think I can." When he reached the top of his mountain, the chant changed to, "I thought I could. I thought I could. I thought I could." The cards and letters had helped keep me climbing, often when I thought the attempt was too much for my engine, too.

Three mornings a week I was still going to physical therapy. Phyllis, now working, wasn't able to take me, so the ladies in the church filled the void, taking me whenever Gary couldn't. Most days, however, he was able to do hospital visiting while I did my physical therapy.

Following my therapy and the days I didn't have sessions, Gary would take me to the church with him; he didn't like to leave me at home alone. He found it easier to keep his mind on his work when he knew exactly where I was and that I was all right. When I was home alone, he worried that I might fall and be unable to get help, so he took me to the church with him and sat me in a chair in his secretary's office. It took all the energy I could muster to just sit in what had become "Sue's chair." Earliene, the church secretary, and Bill Hayes, the minister of maintenance, as Gary fondly nicknamed him, were always so gracious to me. I knew "Sue's chair" was often in their path as they scurried to do their tasks. Earliene never grumbled about "keeping an eye on Sue" while Gary did his work, even when I caused her heart to skip a few beats when I stumbled or almost fell out of my chair, and Bill was well-stocked with fatherly hugs and always a "joke of the day."

My day's energy was soon gone, and Gary pulled me from the chair and took me home for my afternoon nap. I remained in bed until the children came home from school. Then I dragged my heavy body from the bed and collapsed in my reclining chair. Gary would prepare supper, often with Shannon's help, and I was in my reclining chair until the day was over.

Almost daily I called Phyllis. Even though I'm sure

some days she was too busy for the call, she would share in detail the events of her day. This gave me the needed lift during my long uneventful afternoons.

Because of her work schedule, it was difficult for Phyllis to find the time for our walk. Gary and I knew this was a very important part of my recovery, so we continued the daily walks; only we did it in our Dodge City Mall.

When we arrived at the mall,I was so grateful for the handicap sticker my doctor had prescribed. Almost every place we went, there was a parking space reserved for the handicapped. Walking into a building took more effort and energy than I realized. Once inside, I often would have to find a seat to rest from the seemingly long journey from the parking lot. I was learning the value of those parking spaces, especially to those who need them! I hoped those parking in them without permits knew also.

With the debut of fall, the trees began to exchange their green for the colorful wardrobe of orange and red. With this sight my boys would always store away their balls, bats, and baseball gloves for the winter months. The faithful, well-worn ball caps that were removed from their heads only for sleeping and any other time Mom demanded, were retired and thrown on the top shelf of the hall closet.

From their bedrooms they would yell each year, "Where's my football?"

"Have you *tried* looking under your bed?" I would bellow back sarcastically. This year, although our lives were changed in many ways, one thing was the same—my boys were still boys!

Shawn was extremely excited because this would be the first year he would be playing football. His joy knew no limits as my super-slim eighth grader made the team for both offense and defense. As a toddler he had often carried a ball in his hands, wearing a football helmet that rested somewhere between his nose and upper lip.

Shawn loved sports! When he became too old for "Sesame Street," he started watching "Monday Night

Football." His unlimited energy, combined with his dream, like every young boy, to play college ball–football or basketball–gave him the desire to work hard.

We have always tried to encourage our children to pursue their dreams, no matter how bizarre they might sound. Maybe that desire was put there by the Lord Himself. As their parents, we felt responsible to help cultivate or encourage them, and to be there with a needed shoulder for tears if necessary, if their dreams came crashing down. We knew they might fail, but at least they would have tried.

I knew how important football was to Shawn, so it was important to me to try to be there at the games. I felt it was important enough to use any energy I could muster for attending my children's activities, supporting them.

Shawn was to have a football game in Dodge City, and Gary and I began to plan on my going. Summer was making its final pass, and the temperature climbed into the upper nineties the day of the game. Gary was concerned that I might not be able to take the extreme heat, since heat made my symptoms worse. It was a day I didn't have physical therapy, so I spent the entire day resting. I was determined to attend the game.

When we arrived at the stadium, the only shade was on the top row. Hanging on tightly to Gary, I climbed the stairs to the top. As the game started, a breeze began to blow, keeping us cool through the entire game.

Gary pointed to Shawn along the sideline. I could focus on his jersey and see the #89 as long as he stood still, but that only lasted a moment. My vision was still blurred, and it was difficult for me to focus on an object. From the beginning of the game, I didn't know whether Shawn was on the field or on the bench. Gary was getting impatient with my continual questioning, "Where is he now?"

"He got it!" Gary yelled.

"Got what? Who's got it?"

"Shawn just made an interception!" Gary responded.

"I missed it. Oh, well," I sighed," at least I'm able to be here."

As the weather cooled, I attended several more of Shawn's football games. I continued to have a problem keeping track of jersey #89 as it raced on and off the field. Throughout the season, Shawn made several tackles and another interception; I continued to miss it—but at least I was there!

Football season ended and jersey #89 was put to rest with the other jerseys on the team. I sighed in relief and retired to my blue reclining chair for a whole week of rest. My recovery was disturbed as Shawn bounced into the living room yelling, "Mom, I made the basketball team!"

I responded with a somewhat fake, almost glued-on-looking smile, "That's wonderful, Shawn...."

One difference between football and basketball—besides the shape of the balls—was there would now be two or three games a week instead of just one.

I was to discover there were more differences, too, including one concerning the bleachers. Usually during football, the bleachers are stationary or located in a stadium—almost always immovable. In junior high basketball, the bleachers are located in the gymnasium and are usually collapsible, folding against the wall. Before my illness, I hadn't been aware how good one's balance must be to mount one of these things.

Another difference was in the location of the game. In the stadium the cheers of the crowd hadn't bothered me; but in the gym the noise echoed in my head. I was forced to plug my ears in a futile attempt at keeping the noise out.

Also, I found it impossible to move my head from side to side fast enough to keep up with the players. The attempt made me dizzy. It was as if I were moving in slow motion, and they moved at a faster speed. The players were still blurred, although I could focus on them more

123

easily.

Some things, however, remained the same in football and basketball. Just as in the football season, I wasn't always sure if Shawn were in the game. Again Gary tired of my repeated question, "Is Shawn playing?"

As in football, Gary yelled, "He made it!"–followed by my saying, "Who made it? What happened?"

Concerning football and basketball–all I can say is, "I sure missed the instant replays!"

CHAPTER 16

Anne Ratcliffe, a member of our church, took my inability to sing and made it her personal special prayer concern. She believed so strongly that the Lord was going to answer her prayer, she scheduled me to sing at a meeting she was planning for our Pioneer Association.

A retired minister's wife, Jeanne Spencer, also a member of the church, volunteered to give me voice lessons. I was discouraged and frustrated with each extremely flat note as it squeaked out of my mouth. My lips seemed heavy, as I fought the waves of fatigue. The tightness around my chest and face made getting a deep breath impossible. Jeanne constantly encouraged me, mothering me through each lesson.

There was something about Jeanne that made her appearance almost glow. Perhaps it was the result of a life filled with tragedy, and a vital living faith in the Lord, which held her tighter with each situation:

—Jeanne's husband, Chuck, had received injuries which left him disabled. In World War II, the canopy of the plane in which he was a bombardier was shot off, killing the person next to him, and exposing Chuck to temperatures of fifty below zero for four hours.

—A flood in Topeka, Kansas, in 1951 washed away the Spencers' new home and all its contents.

—A plane crash took the life of Jeanne and Chuck's pilot-son, Robin.

—Their only grandchild died, living only a few short weeks.

All these situations, combined with her strong faith in a God who wouldn't let her fall under these trials, gave her a special understanding of others' pain.

When I was around Jeanne, my trial seemed so small! Her warm spirit would make my inner frustration begin to slowly melt away like an ice cream cone on a hot summer's day. If anyone had the ability to encourage me to sing again, it was Jeanne.

I often said during our voice lessons, with my eyes filled with tears, "I can't. It's just too hard!"

With a deep understanding of my painful frustration, she responded, "Yes, you can and you will!" I knew she meant each word!

I was still going to therapy twice a week, and Gary was anxious for me to begin driving the car once again, so I could take myself. I was now able to see well enough to pass the driver's test. It sent a cold shiver up and down my back to realize there were people driving on the streets that couldn't see any better than I could!

I had to work hard to keep my eyes focusing together. My driving would have to be limited to a few blocks around our home—no further than the mile drive to the hospital, driving on all the back streets.

The first time I mounted the seat behind the steering wheel, Gary realized I needed to re-learn the rules of driving. He sat, tightly gripping the door handle, coaching me.

"REMEMBER, you always turn your blinker on when you turn the corner." "SUE, you can't turn a ninety DEGREE CORNER!" "PLEASE hold the steering wheel as steady as possible—THE WEAVING IS MAKING ME SEA SICK..." "YOU'RE DRIVING awfully CLOSE TO THOSE PARKED CARS...!"

Teenagers, I think I understand your problem, as you learn to drive the family car—GOOD LUCK!

There was a brief lull in the hectic basketball schedule for Thanksgiving Day. I was really looking forward to this day with a new and re-born appreciation for life, and an excitement for just being alive. Like the pilgrims, I had much to celebrate and be thankful for.

I wanted to thank the people of our church In Dodge City for all they had done for me and my family, but my mouth still stuck, not allowing the words to flow freely. I felt it would be easier to read them a letter expressing my gratitude.

Although I was doing much better in my walking, I was concerned about climbing the three steps to the pulpit. It might put a damper on everyone's Thanksgiving holiday if I fell as I ascended the stairs. I suggested to Gary that he help me, if he didn't want to create a possibly embarrassing scene. Miss America was not in danger of losing her crown as I made my ascent up the steps to share my letter:

"Dear Family in Christ,

"It's Thanksgiving Sunday and I have something to praise our God for. He has been so gracious to me. He has given me you.

"It is difficult to express what you and your prayer support have meant. There is no way I can thank you for all the things you have done.

"God has given me a mountain to climb, and He definitely will give me the strength to climb it. You have helped me in my climb. I know I will never reach the top of my mountain without your prayers and support.

127

"I have been enveloped in the love of a great God, and the love of friends and family. My mountain has been steep and rough. We serve a wonderful Lord who has given me the strength to climb, as well as friends who often have carried me up my mountain.

"I thank you—with tears of joy. Together, we all—my God, my friends, and I—will reach that mountain top together."

"Love, Sue"

In the letter, many English rules were broken, and several participles left dangling; but there weren't many people left in the congregation without at least moist eyes filled with "tears of joy" and of thanksgiving.

The Christmas lights were being hung as the shoppers rushed from store to store hopeful to find the gifts they desired. To avoid this December rush, my shopping and wrapping were completed by the end of November. All those around me, especially our children, were turning their thoughts toward Christmas. Jason could hardly wait to put up the Christmas tree. I couldn't convince him to forget it just this one year. I could tell Jason had rather strong feelings on the subject, when he said, "No tree—no Christmas!"

Jason's decorating was quite different from my usual precise job. Due to his four-foot height, he wasn't able to reach the top two feet of the tree; but he assured us he didn't want any assistance. When Jason completed the job, he wouldn't let anyone move the decorations. When he completed the tree, it strongly resembled a bald-headed man—bare on top! Jason was happy, and I had to admit, it did bring a little Christmas spirit into our home.

The first week of December, I finished taking all my medication. The doctors had cautioned us that the withdrawal from the Prednisone could be severe, especially since I had been on the drug for six months. My only problems from withdrawal were a slight headache and an inability to cope with the fast pace of Christmas, especially in a minister's family. The holidays were filled with parties and special programs involving the church; this, combined with Shawn's basketball schedule, was causing a "short" in my ability to cope with my life during the holidays. The doctor suggested I leave town, and just drift through the Christmas season.

I was becoming the "scrooge" of our family. The children were in complete agreement with the doctor's decision that it might be better if I spent the Christmas holidays in Topeka with my parents. My family would join me there on Christmas Eve.

The highlight of the holidays for me was a brief trip I took to Wellsville. It was an opportunity for me to share with the people in the Wellsville Baptist Church how my miracle was progressing.

I entered the church on a Sunday night. Prior knowledge of my visit was known only by the secretary, Vesta, and her husband. The church had been responsible for sending up hundreds of prayers for me during the months of my illness. The evening was loaded with hugs filled with love and surprise to see me, as well as tears of rejoicing, as they shared the many thoughts and concerns they had experienced over the past months during my illness.

I also went to the Methodist church, hopeful to find the pastor's wife, my good friend Kathy Baumgartner. The Methodist church was located across the street from the Baptist church. During our eight-year stay in Wellsville, we had made friends on both sides of the street, so walking up the sidewalk to the door of the church filled my thoughts with many memories of living in Wellsville.

As I entered the church, darkened for their Christmas program, Kathy was coming down the stairs with her arms filled with hymn books. I was standing at the foot of the stairs. I called out to her, in fun, "Mrs. Baumgartner."

She descended several more stairs before she recognized me. Throwing the books in the air, she ran down the stairs, wrapped her arms around me, and sobbed. Prepared for her reaction, her husband Allen caught the flying books.

"Kathy, I'm back, I'm back," I said, holding her tightly. I meant I was mentally back from the illness.

She uttered two words in response, over and over: "I know, I know...."

Allen Baumgartner stood by, chanting, "It's a miracle. It really is unbelievable. It's a miracle!"

Allen and Kathy had visited me in the Wichita hospital. To have them so shocked by my progress really reminded me of how far I had come since the onset of my illness, and for a brief moment it helped to pull my thoughts away from how far I still had to climb before reaching the top of my mountain.

Kathy remembered: "When Allen and I went to the Wichita hospital to visit Sue, I was feeling heartsick. What I saw when we entered Sue's room at Wesley Hospital was as bad as I had feared. She looked so small in the bed; she almost looked like Shawn before he began to grow. Sue couldn't focus her eyes; her speech was jerky and sounded high-pitched and childish. Her mom and she were carrying on a conversation which Sue punctuated with funny remarks. Her jokes gave release for the sadness I was feeling.

"When I saw Sue in Topeka this summer, she was better, but still she had a difficult time walking and talking. Her eyes still looked very different. It was hard to see the Sue I knew.

"Then Christmas, 1984, she walked in the door of our church just as I was walking toward it. She looked so super; so pretty, and her natural look was back. Her expression was that of my friend, Sue. I was beginning to believe it was true. Sue was getting well!"

CHAPTER 17

My progress steadily improved over the months that followed, encouraging the faith of everyone watching my recovery; however, the wonder of it wasn't so visible to me and my family. My progress seemed slow as we lived with it on a day-to-day perspective. Those who saw me weekly or monthly viewed it differently. Their reminder of the past weeks and months kept encouraging us.

One Wednesday night, at our monthly church supper a woman, Barbara Morrison, kept staring across the table at me. She finally said. "Sue, I'm sorry to be staring, but I can't help it. When I look at you I get so excited! Everyone here feels that they have in some way had a small part in your miracle."

I thought, everyone there had! Through the past months I could feel their daily prayer support. This church was not the only one supporting me; there were other churches too, from many denominations. My home church, Central United Presbyterian in Topeka, Wellsville Baptist, others I didn't even know about; even First Methodist of Dodge City sent a lay woman from their Stephen's Ministry, Dee Smoll. For almost a year, she made visits to encourage me in my climb. It was exciting to see God's people swarming all over my mountain, offering assistance and support as I continued to climb.

Prayers were not all that was offered. Jason and Shannon, as well as children I didn't even know, were reading books in the M.S. Read-a-thon in my honor. Phyllis' sister, Karen, who walked in an M.S. Walk-a-thon, presented me with her hard-earned T-shirt. The 4-H Club from Wellsville had an all night M.S. Rock-a-thon to earn money as their contribution in our climb. The concern and loving support of all these acts were overwhelming to all my family. I was astonished! So many people had turned the tragedy of my illness into a personal concern.

Anne Ratcliff's prayer finally was answered also. One more item to add to her "praise the Lord list," as she called it. I sang again! On a Sunday evening, the first of March, 1985, one week prior to her special meeting, once again I climbed the stairs to the podium. Gary and our children, Phyllis, Jeanne and Chuck Spencer, Carol, and Anne were among those present. As I looked out into their faces, I knew every person in the audience was more nervous than I, but their supporting looks gave me courage and strength.

The audience and I were aware it wasn't the same quality I had had nine months before, as the many flat notes filled the air, but it was the same joy in my heart filling the room. As I sang, I felt a new source of energy flowing through my body. For one brief moment the heavy burden of the M.S. was lifted from my shoulders.

It would take a lot of work, but somehow deep inside I knew I would be singing again. I felt a peace within my thoughts—my singing might never be the same quality it once was; but I knew, "I must sing! I must sing! I will sing, even if it's just in the shower—where only my ears can be offended!"

Much had been happening within the first year after the M.S. had struck. There were so many new beginnings: each situation—new or old—was as if I had not experienced it before. My life had a new freshness and excitement, much like a rosebud opening one petal at a time, experiencing its birth into nature.

November 10, 1984, I was watching the T.V. As the evangelist was praying, he said, "Someone is being healed from M.S." I began sobbing. I sensed he was talking about me! I felt a confirmation of what I had believed when I was in the hospital in Dodge City—the Lord was going to give me a miracle!

At the same moment, a new friend from the Dodge City church, Linda Fergerson, was flipping through the channels of her T.V. She stopped on the same channel as he began his prayer. She, too, began to believe my promise of a miracle.

My determination, stubbornness, and extreme impatience were beginning to bubble up inside me like a test tube on a Bunsen burner. This is often the formula that erupts when the Lord takes an Irish girl and puts just enough Scottish blood in her to make her dangerous. Knowing He had to put out my "Bunsen burner," the Lord reminded me, in His strong, yet loving voice, "Sue, I said, be patient! Your miracle will come *in MY time!*"

I was unable to escape the questions that surrounded my life daily. "Why me, Lord? Why did you save my life?" I was overwhelmed by the reality that He had saved me, given me life again; but FOR WHAT? I began an earnest daily search for His will. I owed the Lord so much. He gave me life thirty-six years ago. His Son, Jesus, died to save that life, and if that weren't enough... He gave me life again!

July of 1985, a year and a month after my illness, I had an appointment for an examination with the eye specialist in Garden City. I was blessed to have the same technician who had examined my eyes the year before. He was surprised at my progress!

A year before my peripheral vision had been limited to tunnel vision. The technician found upon re-examination that my peripheral vision was completely normal. My vision had tested 20/40 in June, 1984; now, though it took me a few seconds longer than normal to focus my eyes, my vision was 20/20!

I hadn't worn my reading glasses since before the illness. Now, they blurred my vision when the technician had me put them on. I had worn them for the past five years, but my eyes had improved to the degree that I no longer needed glasses!

The technician, also a Christian man, was so excited he was almost jumping up and down. I'm sure everyone else in the office heard his excitement as he shouted, "You've made my whole day! This is such a boost to my faith!"

Gary and I left the office in tears, as we shared the experience. We had struggled many days finding it difficult to continue believing. Was this another way the Lord was telling us I really was experiencing a miracle?

Our oldest daughter, Pam, was married to Todd Oswald on September 14, 1985. I had almost two weeks to survive the experience of being the mother of a bride. I received a call from Annette Aldape about a full-time job as an aide in Central Elementary School working in the English Training Department. I briefly explained to Annette and the principal, Kenneth Friend, what my past year had involved. I didn't know Annette prior to our meeting, but she explained that she, too, was married to a pastor. She already knew of my illness, but she said, "I'm willing to hire you. If you can't do the job, then you'll just have to quit."

She was giving me a chance. Maybe I didn't have the energy to do the job, but she was giving me a chance, even if I failed! I thought to myself, "Lord, I know you have sent this job."

The next day I was in the school putting children on the bus, and the long day was just half over. I was exhausted, feeling I might not even make it through one day. A second-grade teacher, Mary Dunn, came out of her room and said, "Are you the Sue Winget that is a minister's wife?"

I thought there couldn't be another Sue Winget around who meets that requirement. I responded somewhat shyly. "Yes," almost asking a question, not yet sure where this conversation was leading.

"Have you had a serious illness?" she continued.

Feeling as though my life history must be written across my face, I sheepishly answered, "Yes...."

"I've had you on my prayer list for over a year!"

She threw her arms around me and hugged me tightly. With eyes filled with joy, she whispered, "It's a miracle!"

Suddenly the fatigue of the day was easier to bear. I was so filled with gratitude and love to her and to the many other Mrs. Dunns who had also prayed for me.

I responded, "Yes, it is a miracle! Thanks to the prayers of people like you!"

Bill Hayes, the church building engineer, sees me daily. He always greets me with, "Well, how's my miracle girl today!" Over and over he describes first seeing me after I got out of the hospital in Wichita. He continues with extreme seriousness, "You looked so small lying on that couch. I couldn't believe it was you! Now, look at you! My miracle girl!"

....

Gary and I are constantly reminded of my illness wherever we go. One day as Gary saw Dr. Johnson in the hall of the hospital, the doctor repeated once again the words Dr. Barnett, the neurologist from Wichita, had related to him concerning my illness. Dr. Johnson said , "Dr. Barnett hadn't seen a case of M.S. strike so quickly, and so severely." These words brought back to Gary all the memories of a painful period of his life.

As Gary's wife, I knew I could only see the tip of his pain as he spoke of his encounter with Dr. Johnson in the hospital corridor. I encouraged Gary, "Write down what you have learned from my illness." It was difficult to start his list, and it took a lot of wifely encouragement. To his surprise, the thoughts came quickly as he typed them out on the computer.

What I have learned from Sue's illness:

1. God is still alive and living within our family. Many doubt that God is alive. I still have Sue to remind me that God is alive, and working in our world today.

2. Miracles do occur today. Sue's miracle in progress is just one more instance of God's healing power. I wish I had an answer for those whom God does not choose to heal in the way that we think He should. But there is one thing I know. God does heal and perform miracles today. It is by His sovereign will in each case. That does not make healing today any less miraculous!

3. When things get hectic in our life, and we find ourselves at odds with one another, God gently reminds me that I need to be thankful to Him and grateful that I still have Sue. He restored her to health so that we can have a life together.

4. I have more empathy for those that are going through serious illness. When I am involved in counseling or sitting at the bedside of a church member, I can understand what they are going through. Hopefully, I can provide a sense of comfort and understanding to them.

5. I am still searching for answers to why God does not heal and provide the type of miracle that we want. There are so many times I would like to have an answer to give to families as they go through their struggles.

6. I have come to realize that God cannot be programmed. He cannot be confined to one purpose or one method. He is an unlimited God who is carrying out His purpose in our lives. Some remain sick when it is unnec-

essary. We should ask God to heal us. We should pray for the recovery of the sick. But if God says "no" as He said to Paul, or if He says "wait" as He did to the blind man, we should respond with rejoicing and thanksgiving. The ways of God are perfect.

7. God uses various ways to heal and perform miracles. He may choose to do it instantaneously. He may choose to do it gradually. Or He may choose to use medication. I believe that God chose to heal Sue through a gradual process and medication.

8. Finally, I believe that God receives all the credit for Sue's healing. This includes all of the prayers throughout the United States. But through the process He used several doctors and other members of the medical profession. God also used medication. We have shared this with several doctors and members of the medical profession.

"And even we Christians, although we have the Holy Spirit within us as a foretaste of future glory, also groan to be released from pain and suffering. We, too, wait anxiously for that day when God will give us our full rights as his children, including the new bodies he has promised us— bodies that will never be sick again and will never die."

(Romans 8:23 TLB)

....

My reflections over the past year and a half:

High heels have been eliminated from my wardrobe for reasons of balance. Confidentially, I'm glad to have an excuse not to walk on stilts. Grace and elegance were never my virtues!

The Lord promised me a miracle, but He has given me hundreds, maybe thousands. It's easy for me to keep my eyes fixed on my impossible situation, and miss the miracles surrounding me each day, like: three push-ups instead of two; fifty-three typing errors in the A.B.C.'s instead of 162; walking three blocks; cutting my own meat; putting on my socks unassisted...etc.... Each accomplishment is a miracle in itself; each is a part of my miracle in progress.

Illness and trials can put great stress on any relationship. Gary and I were told that ninety-five percent of marriages where one partner is afflicted with M.S. will end in divorce—an awesome statistic! As partners, we knew we had to begin gathering the pieces of our shattered marriage, a difficult and often painful task.

Our children each had to deal with the illness in a different way. Shawn found it easiest since he had been with me through my difficult days in the Wichita hospital. He had seen me at my worst, and knew how far I had come. Jason withdrew completely, finding it too painful to show any affection to me. Shannon couldn't deal with the often painful task of entering her pre-teens, along with the feeling she had lost her "other mother." I hid my feelings of guilt, frustration, even anger concerning my illness, which only complicated our difficult situation.

Tears flood my eyes and my heart aches for each one of us in my family, as I remember all the painful times we have gone through because of the illness. Time will heal our wounds. Sharing our feelings, each hug and word of love brings healing and causes the tears and painful memories to melt like snow.

Bad things will intrude into everyone's life at some unannounced time. It is a fact we can count on! My question must not be, "Why me?" but "How will *I* deal with *my* mountain?"

Jesus Christ has been the guide up my mountain.
He has rescued me from death and anguish.
When I fell from the weight of my load,
He was there to pick me up,
To start me climbing again.
When I keep my eyes fixed on Him,
We will reach the top of our mountain together.
                                        Amen!